THE
ULTIMATE
SALES
MOMENTUM

ANDREW IZUMI

VIRTUAL SUMMIT INTERVIEWS

+ BOX, STUDY GUIDE & CARDS

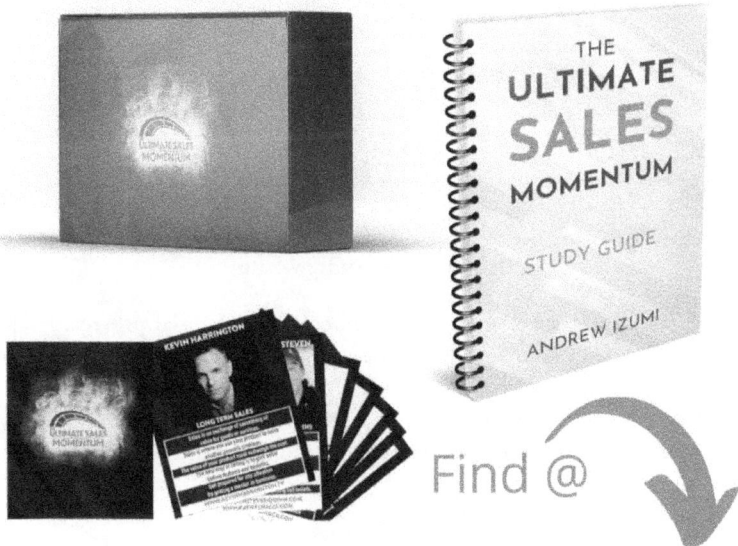

THE
ULTIMATE
SALES
MOMENTUM

STUDY GUIDE

ANDREW IZUMI

Find @

www.ultimatesalesmomentum.com

ISBN: 978-1-64184-301-0

CONTENTS

NOTE TO READER

Welcome. My name is Andrew Izumi, your sales strategist. The Ultimate Sales Momentum is based on eighteen targeted interviews with business and sales professionals. Inside, you will find knowledge from over 250 years of successful business experience using numerous sales tactics to win in business and life. The material inside will show you how I was able to connect with each professional, the sales methodologies they taught during their interviews, and real-life examples of how each tactic was successfully applied. My goal is for you to build your sales momentum as you apply unique skills from each chapter. If you want to reach greater sales heights, apply the teachings in this book immediately and enjoy your success!

THE ULTIMATE SALES MOMENTUM STORY

Welcome to the Ultimate Sales Momentum. My name is Andrew Izumi, your sales strategist. This book is designed to do one thing: teach you various techniques and strategies to achieve sales momentum in your business, professional career, and life. Having sales skills are the #1 most important asset in any business. Whether you are working on closing a large business proposal, working on getting a deal on that sweet new house, or just trying to convince your husband or wife to go to your favorite restaurant, sales skills are essential.

Sales is not about convincing people to purchase something they are not interested in. Rather, it is about ethically persuading someone to see your solution as the vehicle to get them their desired result. As salespeople, it is our duty and responsibility to ensure that the sale is won so the customer can achieve their desired goal or outcome.

Throughout my sales career, I have learned from some of the best, which has allowed me to achieve leading certifications, win global sales contests, and build long term win/win relationships with customers. In this book, I have taken seventeen interviews from billionaires, millionaires, and expert specialists giving you a master guide to building sales momentum in your life. If you are a business owner striving to achieve higher profits, a sales professional who wants to blow past their annual quota, or even someone who is struggling to get the sales ball moving, this book is for you. The strategies inside are time tested and approved by sales leaders across multiple industries.

I wanted to show you why I have chosen to take the time and effort to write this book for your future sales success. At the beginning of my sales career, I struggled time and time again, coming very close to giving up. Through learning from the best of the best, I was able to close deals and make plenty of money. It wasn't always this way, though. It took many years before achieving any notable success.

My college education was in engineering management. I had no desire to become a sales professional as I was an introvert and the thought of talking to people for a living scared the living daylights out of me. I had friends, but I was no relationship expert or the popular kid in school. There was no gift of gab for me. If I could stay behind a computer, crunch the numbers, and make a decent predictable salary, I would be a happy engineering graduate.

I graduated in 2009, and in the United States, our economy had taken a turn for the worst. I had always dreamed of working for a Boeing, Northrop Grumman, Lockheed Martin, or another defense contractor. But there were no paying positions open the year I graduated. I vividly remember looking on job boards only to see the words "no open positions" written for every single position. My search would continue to the section for unpaid internships. Again, I found those same words "no open positions" written on not once, not twice, but for every company I wanted to apply to. My heart sank as I now realized that those long, sleepless nights studying physics and differential equations weren't going to benefit me one bit.

At this point, I had a choice. I could go back to school and get my master's degree, paying more money and spending more time in a lab. Or, I could get the only job that was hiring at the time: sales. I was thrown into the fire with little training, left to sink or swim. In the beginning, I was barely able to tread water. Soon after, I started sinking. As soon as this happened, I knew that I needed to learn from others who were already successful. After many introductions, handshakes, and lunches bought for others, I grew my network and had others teaching me how to sell. My sales skills very quickly went from novice to average and then to expert.

The key for my success was to continue to learn from the best of the best. Soaking up all the best knowledge allowed an engineering student to be successful in the world of sales. I was even able to win the Rainmaker Program at a Fortune 500 company. And yes, that year I was able to make it rain with sales and commissions.

At this point, I thought to myself, *How can I help others achieve the same sales success so they do not have to go through the years and tiring experience of finding and learning from the experts in the field?* This is when the Ultimate Sales Momentum was born. My network has been growing year after year, and if I could share this experience and knowledge with others this would be very fulfilling. I looked at my "Rolodex" of contacts and targeted seventeen unique experts to interview. I wanted to target five main segments:

1. The Cornerstone Foundations of Sales
2. A Sales Superior Mindset
3. Strategies and Systems for Success

4. Being Confidently Aware Of Your Situation
5. Online and In-Person Tactics

In the chapters ahead, I am confident that I will help any salesperson magnify their results significantly in business and life. Each chapter is written from lessons that are learned from experts and also include their personal stories. These virtual interviews can be found at www.ultimatesalesmomentum.com.

I asked each interviewed expert these targeted questions:
- Can you tell me what sales mean for you in your business, more than just money?
- What is your most jaw-dropping sales story?
- Can you give any actionable advice to help readers build sales momentum in business now?
- What is the most difficult sale you have had?

I have two main goals for this book:
1. To teach you proven strategies that will result in win after win.
2. To connect each reader with the speakers and myself, so if further education is desired, you have credible sources to turn to.

I know this information will be life changing. Please enjoy the stories and strategies ahead. I look forward to sales not only becoming a profitable activity but also an enjoyable and fulfilling part of your life.

CORNERSTONE FOUNDATIONS

There are four cornerstones to sales and it is important to start with the foundation. In sales, there is short-term and long-term thinking. When you focus on short-term thinking, you are left fighting for each and every sale This does bring quick success, but it can be short-lived. If we focus on the long-term, then you will be amazed at how well your business will perform for many years into the future.

Thinking long-term is not only critical for yourself, but for your customer's success as well. There was once a manufacturing solution I had for a customer, The Wonderful Company. (And yes, this is the name of the company.) The Wonderful Company was working on a sorting line for Halos Oranges. Our solution was three times as expensive as the competitor's product, took longer to receive and design, but would end up saving the customer twenty times as much as the cost of our product. We spent our time working with their team to engineer the perfect solution, and it ended up being a big win/win for everyone. The customer saved a lot of money, and I won the sale. The best thing was that, once I won the sale, I never had to worry about a competitor stealing away my business. I was locked in and sold myself as a long-term partner.

One aspect that I used to win this business and stay profitable was knowing my numbers. It is critical to know the cost of your product, how much you can sell, and how many repetitive orders you will receive. Furthermore, when I was able to calculate these same numbers for my customer, giving them an estimated ROI (Return on Investment), I was able to ethically persuade them to purchase my product.

I am an engineer by education and have always enjoyed math and science, so it was simple for me to play to my strengths in arithmetic. Knowing that I had the ability to make a mathematical calculation, when my competitors were trying to persuade the customer with overplayed lunches and donuts, gave me a distinct and unique advantage.

This sales win stemmed from listening to the customer, and The Wonderful Company told me exactly how they needed to be sold. I could tell that my competitors were not able to prove to them a long-term monetary solution. As I listened to my customer talk about their hardships and future goals, they gave me the ammunition to know exactly how to focus the sale.

In these four upcoming chapters, you will find these techniques explained by masters in the sales field. From billionaires to top-ranked professional sales speakers, enjoy the stories and lessons ahead.

LONG-TERM SALES

Kevin Harrington

An original "shark" on the hit TV show *Shark Tank*, the creator of the infomercial, pioneer of the As Seen on TV brand, and co-founding board member of the Entrepreneur's Organization, Kevin Harrington has pushed past all the questions and excuses to repeatedly enjoy 100X success.

T he first interview I had scheduled for the Ultimate Sales Momentum was with Kevin Harrington, who is widely known as the 5 Billion Dollar Man. (That's billion with a capital B.) It took me some time to get connected with Kevin, but when I did, he was able to provide a lot of value that I've included in this book. I was so blessed to have his knowledge and talent here on the Ultimate Sales Momentum.

Initially, I was a little intimidated because I didn't know what to think about talking to someone of his caliber, but he was down to earth—just a good, kindhearted gentleman. I had been working on this relationship for about six months when I decided to invest in a course with James Smiley. I was given the chance to have a group chat with Kevin that was of immense value. During the next group chat, I asked if he was willing to do an interview. He agreed, and I was super ecstatic because I knew he had so much value to give to people who would be reading this book.

Originally, I was thinking about just having the interview and sharing what I learned with everyone, but I ended up connecting with Seth Greene, who's a sponsor for this book's virtual event and a co-host of the podcast *The SharkPreneur* with Kevin Harrington. Seth was also a part of my past virtual summit, Summit Ignite.

When I talked to Seth, he said, "You did such a great job putting on Summit Ignite, and because you have this interview coming up with Kevin, we should really try to get this all into a virtual summit. Not to mention that you've been an expert in sales for over the past ten years. Kevin Harrington purchased the rights to Zig Ziglar's, *Secrets of Closing the Sale*, so this virtual summit could be a great way of providing sales value to the audience as well as a chance for you to be successful yourself."

It took some time to get everything scheduled, but I was able to work with the Ziglar family company. During the interview, I learned some very important foundational pieces that are incredibly vital for anybody.

What you should know is that Kevin Harrington, the As Seen On TV pioneer, is actually the inventor of the infomercial, just like the ones with the George Foreman grill. He's also the original shark from the hit TV show *Shark Tank*. Kevin's first sale was made all the way back in the '60s. I learned from him that sales is simply an exchange of something of value for goods or services.

Money doesn't always equate to success. Some companies are good at raising a ton of money, but they have no sales so they're not cash positive. You need sales in order to grow a business and to sustain it. Once, Kevin was flying into Saudi Arabia and wanted to sell to a company, RT, Arabian Radio TV. This company runs all the television operations in all twenty Arab countries. He was selling RT to put his infomercials on every channel. And what we need to learn from this is very, very interesting.

Before Kevin even started with the pitch, he told the company he was in discussions with some of their competitors, as a disclaimer. They then immediately explained to Kevin why they were better than all of their competitors. Kevin went into this thinking he was going to need to be prepared to pitch this product and try to convince them to buy it—but surprisingly, the reverse happened.

They brought in their whole team to meet with Kevin and said, "We're the best out of all of our competitors, and we need to convince you ours is the best network." The whole team was trying to convince Kevin why he needed them, why he needed to choose them to put his infomercials on their TV networks. That same day—in just in *one* day—Kevin walked out with a $25 million sale. He had learned this technique from one of his mentors, the great Zig Ziglar.

Zig Ziglar wrote a book called *Secrets of Closing the Sale*. Kevin wrote version two of the book when Zig passed away, and he now works with the Ziglar family. One of the secrets to closing the sale here is the fear of loss, which is exactly what Kevin used in Saudi Arabia. For clarity, that company was thinking, *Are we going to lose out on something if we don't go with Kevin? I don't know why Kevin wants to go with any of our competitors. I know he's talking to them, but we're the best.* They did not want to lose out on this opportunity. Also, they had unused hours of airtime that they could utilize with infomercials and make millions of dollars, which indeed they did.

One of the other things that we've learned is that there are several different types of salespeople. Some people are aggressive and more focused on the short-term, while others concentrate on the long-term and are focused on helping the customer get what they want. The great Zig Ziglar said, "You can get everything in life that you want if you can just help enough people get what they want." That is exactly what the long-term sale looks like.

When we look at sales, at the core of it, we understand that the product has to solve other people's problems. As long as the benefit of your product outweighs the cost, you should be able to sell that product. You need the value of your product to be more than the price, but if the value does not exceed the price, it will be very hard to close the sale. What you want to do in that situation is to start stacking the value. Give another feature, another benefit, or maybe even another product until you increase the value above the price.

Kevin gave us two pieces of actionable advice, one of which is to read *Secrets of Closing the Sale*. There are so many secrets to closing the sale. What you can gain is the knowledge of sales tactics that were relevant in the past and those that are currently relevant. This will teach you the difference between the old and the new ways. The old way was more to push features and benefits, to tell people exactly why they needed to buy the product, how it would benefit them, etc. And the new way is just to give *value*.

For example, Kevin told us about this company BarkBox, who has tens of thousands of people taking videos of opening their boxes. It's a box that gets delivered to your home with dog toys and treats. Since they had so many valuable videos, they were able to give those all out to the public. BarkBox then had customers who bought in because they wanted more of that type of product and emotion in the video. You can start closing sales when people feel they've already received so much value in the front end, and that is the new way of selling.

One of the other big pieces of actionable advice that Kevin taught us was to make sure you get a mentor in business. Mentors can shortcut your path to success and tell you how to avoid business landmines and road blocks. Having a mentor in business is having somebody who has already been down that road and has seen all the land mines, maybe even stepped on one or two. A mentor is like having a guide who's holding your hand. They have that map of how to get from point A to point B without falling into traps. Traps won't disappear; they'll always be there. But you want somebody to guide you down that road to success without succumbing to those traps.

When I concluded my conversation with Kevin, he said the most difficult sale he ever had was getting his wife to marry him. Now, in the beginning, she didn't want to have anything to do with him. Kevin is really a hard-charging business man. But she wanted to know that there was a 'warm and fuzzy' side of Kevin, and it took him three years to finally close the deal. He now has a very happy family.

To connect with Kevin Harrington, please visit:
https://kevinharrington.tv

YOUR NUMBERS' RELATION TO YOUR PROFIT

Anthony Powell

An affiliate marketing legend, Anthony had the privilege of being personally mentored directly and indirectly by the best success coaches in the industry. One being Jim Rohn, world-renowned business philosopher, who was responsible for training legends like Anthony Robbins.

I was extremely impressed when I looked up information about Anthony Powell, which includes his strategies, accomplishments, and how he'd been crowned the king of affiliate marketing. I checked out his mastermind class and knew he had a very solid sales strategy.

We performed a short interview during the holidays, and Anthony was kind enough to give us some very solid golden points on sales. He explained that sales can be a world where people get choked up, but it doesn't have to be this way. Sales is truly connecting with people to give them what they want. When you come into the sale knowing what your customers want, it's very easy to sell. The other aspect we have to think about is we always want to under-promise and over-deliver. Never over-talk the sale because you might talk customers out of it.

Don't under-talk the sale either, which means not giving the customer enough information so they fully understand the product. In sales, we develop a relationship with our customers and it's all about connecting with those individuals. When we're looking out for the best interest of the customer, you'll always sell the correct way and with integrity. If we don't have the proper product for the customer, it doesn't do us any good to sell them.

Anthony makes a great analogy with sales and fly fishing. In sales, you want to be able to explain your product well to your customer. In fly fishing, you want to be able to throw your line in the water, but you want your fly to hit the water before your line. This is so the fish focuses on the fly first. Do not lay the line down and have the fly hit the water last. When this happens the fish is scared away because it focuses on the line instead of the fly. It works the same way in sales. You want to have that core customer focus first, which is like the fly, and then lay down the line afterward, which grabs the customer into the sale.

Come into your sales presentation with certainty, then give the customers exactly what they came for. Your customers will know when you have ownership over what you're talking about, and those specific situations will lead to sales.

Anthony's most jaw-dropping sales story was back in 2010 before today's robust webinar platforms existed. He had patched together multiple webinar softwares to promote his brand and got 6,000 people on a single webinar. In a period of 45 minutes, he was able to create about $1.2 million worth of sales. It's vital to come into the sales presentation with certainty, which will allow you to give your customers exactly what they came for. Through Anthony's webinar he was certain that using multiple softwares and presenting to a large audience was going to be successful. During the sales conversation, your customers will know if you have ownership of what you're talking about. We learn that only then will they buy from you.

The traditional way of selling is by picking up the phone, running an ad in a newspaper, and making cold calls and closing sales. This is merely a numbers game. According to Anthony, this is the old way of selling. You get a specific number of closes per a specific number of leads.

The new way of selling is by using a sales funnel. The sales funnel takes customers through a series of steps to get the most qualified customers to come out the back end and purchase your product. These series of steps can now be automated with technology. What's amazing is that once Anthony started utilizing sales funnels in his business, his sales increased by 1,000%!

Today, we can capture somebody's name and email address on an online platform, then run them through a series of value pieces and questions to qualify them. This makes sure they are the ideal customer for the sale. We can then get them on the phone and close the sale. This will increase our conversion rates because when we get customers on the telephone and spend quality sales time and effort; we only want to talk with people who are most likely to buy.

Know the numbers. Know the conversions for each part of your sales funnel. The conversions are how many leads it takes for you to get an opt-in and how many of those opt-ins it takes for you to get a sale. This result is finding your cost per acquisition on each lead. On the phone, calculate the same thing. Calculate how many leads you get. How many outbound dials you do. How many script reads are done by the salesperson. Finally, how many are closed sales. This gives you your closing ratio. When you're able to measure these pieces, you find out the exact part of the sales funnel you need to fix.

Anthony gives all his sales guys the same proven script. When it comes down to it, it's not what's on the script that's working, it's how they're saying it. We have to remember that people buy from people. They don't want to hear the pitch. You want the customer to get value over the sales call and then present them with the offer.

Anthony has two pieces of actionable advice. First, pick a product that is scalable. Go after abundance and make a lot of money. The product should really sell itself in the way you present it. If you pick a product that's scalable, and it sells itself, it will be very easy when asking for the money. And when you ask for the money, you'll have that confidence to assume the sale and assume the close. This way you're not going into your sales conversation and leaving the sales close open-ended.

Next, sell products that people have to reorder every month. We call this continuity, residual income, or passive income. We need to ask ourselves questions about this specific product. Is it in high demand today? Will it be in high demand twenty years from now? The one thing we don't want to do is to have to keep rebuilding our products and try to sell them again and again, always having to start over from ground zero. These continuous products will build you residual income, so you don't have to keep hustling and working repeatedly for the sale.

For instance, when you're in real estate, you sell a house and receive a large 1 time commission. But next time you have to start over with new houses to sell. If you have something like software that people get value from, you can have them pay a monthly fee. These orders will come each and every month. For as long as people continue to need your product, you will have that income. The great thing is if you want to become even more wealthy, you just sell more products and it will grow exponentially.

Anthony talked about the most difficult sale he's had. This occurred in the very beginning of his business when he was pitching to his best friend to move out to Seattle, Washington to work on a startup with him. His best friend was a successful CPA, had stock options with the company he worked for, was making about a half million dollars a year, and had a wife and kids. Anthony pitched him the numbers and eventually convinced him to move out to Washington and start their business.

When they got to Washington, they took over a business that was making $30,000 but had $40,000 in bills. Through some persistence, they sold a copy machine to get a little money, then turned that business around. Anthony was confident from day one that they would be successful. Now, their business is making $30 million. This was Anthony's toughest sale, but it came from the confidence of knowing how to sell and how to acquire leads.

To connect with Anthony Powell, please visit:
http://www.anthonypowell.com

STRENGTH-FINDING KINGS AND QUEENS

Kevin Steven and Kathy Walls

Kevin spent over twenty-five years in the corporate space, managing large sales teams for manufacturing companies. Kevin and his sales teams have closed over two billion dollars in revenue over his corporate career. Kevin also managed business development for the largest affiliate digital marketing company on the planet with close to 800,000 affiliate marketers.

Kathy Walls is an e-commerce and affiliate marketer who got her start on the Etsy platform with a print-on-demand business. She was able to scale her hobby into a six-figure business.

I've had a working relationship with Kevin Steven and Kathy Walls for a long time now. Kevin and I met early in 2019 through another virtual summit that I hosted called Summit Ignite. He spoke on the topic of sales, as he has been a very successful sales manager and salesman. He provided tons of value for the summit on that topic and was able to help the audience learn so much. After the summit, I kept in touch with Kevin. We chat about life, business, and everything in between. He's been a very kind individual to the entrepreneur space as well as to me, offering up advice and even in-person parties for people to network and have a good time over a beer and BBQ.

Kathy Walls and I met in a group coaching program. We connected inside of a small group, where we met weekly for about 60 to 90 minutes and discussed business. She and I connected because I saw that she was an honest person who worked hard, had a seven-figure e-commerce business, and knew we could ultimately help each other out. Since then, Kathy and Kevin have gone into business together in some different respects, one of them being podcasting and the other a business group coaching program. I've kept in touch with this power team, and we've bounced ideas off each other, grown our inner relationships within the community, and have brought our businesses to the next level.

Kathy explained that selling is delivering your products to your own specific niche while providing value. Throughout the process, you need to find the problems and sell the solutions to your customers. In Kevin's opinion, sales is the lifeblood of the company. Without sales, the company has no life. A surprising statistic is that 90% of small businesses don't even make it past year one, which means they don't graduate into year two because they have no sales. It doesn't matter whether you're in a small business, if you're a solopreneur, a large corporate Fortune 500 company—if you don't have sales, there will be no marketing manager, manufacturing plant, engineering team, or other departments in the company. You need all those other departments because they are necessary to run your business, but it starts with a successful sales team. And it's not only the titled salespeople. Everybody in the company is a member of the sales team because everybody in the company is driving that sale forward.

Another interesting fact is that sales is about hunting and farming. This means that you have to acquire your customer. But after you acquire a customer, it isn't just a one-time action with no follow up. It's imperative that you follow up with your customers and keep giving them value. You need to take care of them with all of their problems and questions. The nice thing about this is that after you've already paid the cost to acquire a new customer, you can continue to sell them products. Whether you sell them a product over continuity, which is a monthly subscription, or you sell a customer a single product you can keep selling value. You can also continually sell them new products as you bring them through your value ladder. This is giving them something small in the beginning, then something a little bit better, then something a little bit more involved, etc. Within that process, the price rises each time.

Kevin had an example of this. He used to be employed in corporate America and was working with school districts selling them products. He came in during a project with a very aggressive price to get into business with the school district. Once he was in, he had a software product that was packaged over a three-year agreement. On their initial product sale, their profit margin was around 30%. But on their three-year subscription software product, which they sold for $8 million, it was almost pure profit at 90%. This is an example of continuing to sell your customers after they have already bought. You'll benefit long after that first customer acquisition or sale.

Kathy was telling us that she was working with a client who was in his own way. He just didn't want to sell his product. Maybe he felt like a sleazy used-car sales guy and didn't want to feel the pressure of selling. She convinced him to just go out there, sell his product, and get paid what he was worth. The second time he pitched his product, he closed a $10,000 sale, which he had not done previously because he was scared to sell it.

Kathy's example shows that you need to go and try to sell, even if you don't think you're any good. Don't be scared of selling or being rejected because, the more you try to sell, the more you're going to learn. In the end, the more you're going to profit because you'll get better and better as long as you're self-diagnosing and improving. You'll never achieve greatness if you can't get out of the gate.

Kevin's secret to success is the power of connecting. If someone has a need, then you either sell them a product that will get them the desired solution or connect them with an individual who can get them to the solution. This is also known as the ripple effect. As soon as you make an impact with one person, that impact will ripple throughout your circle. Whether it's through a friend of a friend or another colleague, this ripple effect will make a positive impact in your life and your business. It may not be a direct contact. It may be a third or fourth-degree relationship, but it will come back positively to you.

When you help people, always know in the back of your mind that through that connection and through that relationship, you're actually really helping yourself. Kevin's strength is connecting. He found his strength in a book called *StrengthsFinder*. Per the book, Kevin realized that, when he connected with people and matched them to their strengths, played to their talents, and highlighted their positive qualities, he got much more done than merely trying to improve upon their weaknesses. Also, when you play to somebody's strengths, their weaknesses will gradually decrease. This is very critical especially in management.

Kathy emphasized the importance of getting inside your own head and identifying your strengths. If you don't know what your strengths are, it's very hard to grow. Doing this will only allow you to be more powerful and effective when you're confident.

Kathy's pieces of actionable advice are to know what you're selling, as it's extremely important to know what your product is and how it's going to positively affect your customer. Also know who you're selling your product to. There are a lot of people in the corporate space or the entrepreneur space who don't exactly know who their customers are and are guessing which products their customers will need. Think as if you were your own customer. With that kind of thinking, you'll craft a fantastic product.

Regarding the notion of selling, always remember that, until you can get over your limiting self-beliefs, it's impossible to succeed. I'm not talking about in the beginning before you even know what you're selling. I'm talking about getting out there, asking questions, and getting some answers. If people are telling you that your questions aren't relevant, you need to ask different questions. Some people will tell you what they think you should offer, which is going to tell you what and to whom you're selling. Remember, the more you get out there and the more you ask questions, the more comments and answers you get. This results in the more you'll know what you're selling and who you're selling to.

Kevin gives us two actionable items. One is to get the *StrengthsFinder* book.

You can find this book on Amazon here: www.ultimatesalesmomentum.com/strengthsfinder

Find your core strengths and play to those strengths, not to your weaknesses. The second one is to get a coach. It doesn't have to be an in-person coach, but some sort of continuing education possibly in the form of podcasts, a book, online course, etc. What we've known for many years of selling is that we all have something we can learn from somebody else. People have been in your shoes before, and it's valuable when you can learn from someone who's had the experience.

Kevin's hardest sale outside of business was his wife. He didn't really have his stuff together before he asked this "smokin' hot blonde," a college cheerleader, to marry him.

It was a difficult sale because she came from a family with money and he didn't. All he had was his beat-up Mazda. However, he was still able to make the sale. It was an interesting experience because Kevin's wife taught him a lot about who he was and who he now is today. She taught him that he needed to value himself more.

When they were living in Houston back in the 90s, Kevin was making $35,000 a year. She eventually called Kevin out and told him that he was worth more than what he thought he was. An offer presented itself to him, and he had a chance to fly out to Milpitas, California to meet with a Taiwanese manufacturer. From what they discussed and agreed on, he went from a salary of $35,000 a year to a job that paid over $100,000 a year, plus a bonus in commission. After this opportunity came, so did another and another and so on. He was able to grow and keep growing.

Kathy's most difficult sell was to actually sell herself. When she and her husband, Scott, were in their early 20s, they only had about $5,000 in the bank. They had two small kids and were on their path to entrepreneurship, but they didn't know if they could do it. They had to sell to themselves that they could go out there and start a business. It was a risky situation. They sold themselves successfully and were given a $50,000 loan that turned into over a million dollars worth of sales in just 18 months.

To connect with Kevin Steven, please visit:
http://www.kevinstevenquinn.com

To connect with Kathy walls, please visit:
https://www.kathylwalls.com

RAPID GROWTH THE LAZY WAY

Matthew Pollard

Matthew Pollard is responsible for five multi-million-dollar business success stories in his home country of Australia, all before the age of thirty. His humble beginnings, the adversities that he faced, and his epic rise to success are inspirational stories of how anyone, with the right motivation and the right strategies, can achieve anything they set their mind to.

I met Matthew Pollard through Seth Greene from SharkPreneur. Matthew and I spoke on the phone to see if this was a mutually beneficial project for him to be a part of, and I learned that he had become a master at selling as an introvert. When I watched Matthew's videos, as I was intrigued to find out more about how he was able to master sales as an introvert because I am one as well. In one of his videos, he said he was able to move from being a very beginner salesman to the top-selling salesman within the large company he worked for and in a very short period of time. I had to find out exactly how he was able to do this, and Matthew was kind enough to bless us with his presence on the Ultimate Sales Momentum.

For Matthew, sales is derived from the Scandinavian word meaning "to serve." It's our job to get our clients over their own mental blocks from purchasing the product you have to sell. Once we're able to get our customers past these mental blocks, we can successfully serve them. Most people don't want to be sold to and most salespeople don't want to "sell." It's imperative for you to move from being the salesperson, which is more argumentative and con-fronting, to a consulting individual, which is much more advice-based. This is similar to an accountant or a doctor.

If you're a good salesperson, you owe it to your cus-tomer to help them make a decision on day one with the product that suits them. Nobody wants to talk to multiple salespeople. If your customer is able to make the decision on day one, it helps avoid the hassle of having multiple conversations. You're actually doing your customer a favor by selling them properly if you do so from the very begin-ning. Furthermore, the customer doesn't run the risk of running into a bulldog salesperson, who would be very slick at selling them a product that may not be a good fit.

When sales is done right, your customer will almost feel dumb if they do not move forward with purchasing your product. To do this, it's essential that you know your customer inside and out. Know what they need to succeed with and what their problems are. This is essential. When you're proving to your customer that you're able to help them, you also need to prove to them that you've helped out other people that are just like them—because in business, everybody thinks they're different.

It is important to be able to speak to that specific individual, and you do this by starting with a specific niche. You can always branch out to a more general market later. But with that specific niche, you'll understand all the customers' problems and you can sell directly to those problems. For example, it's like the difference between going to a doctor who's a general practitioner and one who's a specialist. When you go to a general practitioner, you wonder if they're going to give you the right diagnosis, and you don't know if you're going to get what you need. But when you go to a specialist, you give them your full trust that they know what's going on with your specific issue. By understanding our customers, that is how we need them to feel—like they are going to make a safe decision when buying from us.

Matthew told me he doesn't like when sales are not done right. He also doesn't care for people giving him the response, "Well, things have always been done this way." When he hears that, his natural reaction is to ask why. If things have always been done a specific way, do they continually need to be done that way? For instance, if traditionally it needs to take six to twelve months to close a corporate deal, why does it always have to be within that time frame? It doesn't take that long for Matthew. He is often able to make the sale right on the spot with corporate clients.

The greatest part is being able to overcome the fact that things have always been done a certain way and then break the mold. When you have a rock-solid sales process, you're able to make the purchasing decision feel comfortable for the customer. One way to do this is by telling stories. Do something other than creating artificial rapport. When we don't sell stories in our sales pitch, we can kill the sale and confuse the customer by over pitching or over selling, which can make the customer feel uncomfortable.

For instance, if I told you to remember three words—chair, porridge, bed—and repeat it back to us at the very end of this book, there's a very low likelihood that you'd be able to do it. But if I told you the story of *Goldilocks and the Three Bears* where she sat in a chair, ate some porridge, and slept in a bed; you'd be able to remember those three items. One fantastic thing inside of a sales presentation is to ask specific questions of the customer that naturally lead you into stories. This makes your customers feel comfortable and leads them down the road to a purchasing decision.

Matthew explained his sales process, one that's specifically for introverts. His methodology involves systems and continuous improvement. There is a difference between introverts and extroverts. Extroverts believe they have the gift of gab. They can wing the sales conversation enough to win, have a different conversation every time, and they don't need to go into a conversation with a predefined plan. Introverts will spend more time listening to the customer. They understand the need to follow a process and hold on to this process for dear life because it's what is used for guidance. With repetition, they'll improve the process and start getting more sales.

Extroverts know they need to listen more, so they'll find help or coaching for this. Introverts believe they don't have the gift of gab and may feel a little inferior. One sales methodology Matthew uses is building rapport. There's no need to walk into a sales conversation and strike up a conversation about a random picture hanging on the wall. If you understand how conversations are normally structured, and you have predefined responses to specific questions, then you can systematically and predictably build rapport.

For instance, we know that when we have sales conversations in an office setting, we'll often be offered coffee or water. When Matthew is offered coffee, he can strike up a conversation by saying, "I've already had a few coffees today and if I have another one, I'll just be bouncing off the walls. I actually found that by drinking too much coffee, I have too many ups and downs during the day. Now, I drink matcha tea, which gives me a steady level of energy throughout the whole day." What this does is strikes up an interesting conversation with any caffeine or non-caffeine drinker to automatically build rapport.

Also, when you build rapport, you always want to make sure that you're striking up a positive conversation. Matthew is Australian, and many people have asked him about the Australian fires that went on during the winter of 2019. He is systematically able to understand that he needs to cater his response to build positive rapport because nobody wants to start a conversation off with negativity.

The second thing you want to do is set the agenda for the meeting. Make sure to ask your customers specific questions and provide them with an offer at the end.

The third step is to qualify the person you're selling to. When you walk into an office or talk to somebody on the telephone, you don't want to sell to the receptionist, even though they are a very important person. Don't spend all your time in the office selling to the wrong person when they aren't even the one who can make the purchasing decision. Ask the receptionist a few questions to figure out how to get to the decision-maker by still allowing them to feel like they're important.

Always know what questions to ask during the sales presentation to get your desired result. The goal of asking questions is to become the only logical choice for the customer to purchase from. Another way to be the only logical choice is to separate yourself from the competition. Be extremely unique with the offer you make to the customer.

Matthew has two pieces of actionable advice. First, believe that you can sell well, especially if you're an introvert. Have the belief that you can be a great salesperson. The great Zig Ziglar was an introvert, and there are many other successful salespeople who are introverts as well. Also, you need to believe in yourself. When Matthew first went into sales, he tried to find a job during the holidays and the only types of jobs that were accepting people were sales jobs. So Matthew obtained a commission-based sales job. He was not very good at it, to begin with. Initially, it was difficult having to talk to nearly a hundred people just to get one sale. He was ecstatic after his first sale until he realized he had to do it all over again the next day, and the following day, and the day after that.

Matthew believed that he could do it, but needed a better way. He looked up sales strategies on YouTube and tried to figure out exactly how he was going to improve his skills. Eventually, one hundred conversations to get a sales turned into seventy, which turned into fifty, then forty, and so on. This continued until he was able to get a sale repeatedly with far fewer sales conversations than before.

At this time, Matthew was working at the number one sales and marketing firm across the Southern Hemisphere. One day, his manager pulled him into the office and told him that he was the number-one ranked salesman across the whole country, out of thousands of people, and was up for a management position. As he got started with management, he went on YouTube to learn how to manage. His goal was to get better and better at it. The moral of the story is that you need to believe that you can sell and do it well. Then keep working at it to improve day in and day out.

The second piece of actionable advice is to go into your sales conversation with a specific structure. This will allow you to focus, not on what you have to say next, but on the customer and their reactions during the conversation. When you have a structure in place, you know immediately what needs to come next. This way, you can be in the present moment and observe what the customer is doing.

One other tip Matthew left us with is that once you have your structured sales system, if you want to change something within it, only change one thing at a time. Treat the sales system like a science project. One specific change can make a dramatic difference in your results, either positive or negative. By only making one change at a time, you'll know exactly which changes are successful and those that are not.

Matthew's hardest sale that he made outside of his business was himself. And this is not only just true for him but for most people as well. Studies have proven that daily we tell ourselves up to 60,000 stories of why we can't do something. And if you're an introvert, it's your nature to self-criticize. Stop telling yourself you can't do things because, if you think you can't do them, that will become your reality. There's a quote from Henry Ford that says, "If you think you can, or if you think you can't, you're right." Matthew suggests setting small attainable goals. Don't set too many of those big outrageous goals because you could set yourself up for failure. Start small and build up confidence by accomplishing them.

According to Matthew, it's at every minute and every second you get to choose who you are and what you believe in. This means that you do have control over your life. You have the choice of what you want your life to be like. You can make your sales success and business success a reality.

To connect with Matthew Pollard, please visit:
http://matthewpollard.com/growth

SUPERIOR MINDSET

Any salesperson can succeed when they understand both their personal mindset and their customer. It is just as important to understand yourself as it is to understand your customers. At the beginning of 2019, I was selling for two different influencers. One was a sales funnel builder and the other was a software designer. There was a huge difference between them, and I have to admit that I was only successful with one client.

I made the mistake of taking on the software client, but the sales funnel client was superb. The difference was a 0% close rate and a 50% close rate for online sales calls. The extreme difference from horrible to superb was due to a few factors with my mindset.

The first factor was that I knew everything about the sales funnel customer because I had been one before. Sales funnels were ingrained in my sales DNA, so I understood what was going on in the customer's mind during the sale. The objections were very clear, and I could work on overcoming them before any questions even arose. Furthermore, once potential customers knew that I had personally been in their shoes, natural rapport was built and there was a sense of trust.

This sales experience was so great, that I even work with this funnel builder today on my projects. You can see his work at www.ultimatesalesmomentum.com. He was happy to be a client of mine, and I got a chance to become a client of his as well.

When focusing on both you and your customer's mindset, it is imperative to be truthful to yourself. Once you are truthful to yourself, you can be honest with your customer and get them the results they deserve. We are going to take a deeper dive into why we are selling and the inner workings of the mind during the sales process. Keep distractions away while you are reading these chapters. The upcoming content will blow your mind and is worth reading several times.

YOUR CUSTOMER'S INNER MIND

Tim Shurr

Tim is transforming the way leaders, sales professionals, and entrepreneurs communicate with themselves, their teammates, strategic partners, and customers. As an expert in human behavior and communication, Tim has facilitated over 10,000 coaching sessions and discovered how to quickly shift the unconscious habits that hold people back from having a greater impact.

I had a chance to meet Tim Shurr through Christopher Vos. Christopher and I had such a fantastic interview that I asked him if he had any other suggestions on individuals that would be perfect for the summit. Christopher said he had a friend named Tim who speaks on the mindset and hypnosis of sales. I was very intrigued to be able to talk with him. During the time that I was trying to get connected, Tim was on an awesome vacation at Disney World, and as soon as he came back, I was anxious to get on the phone with him. When speaking with this highly intelligent gentleman, I knew I had to get him on the summit.

According to Tim, sales is a process of helping people get to their goal by finding a way to eliminate the pain they have and moving them toward pleasure. Your customers know you care about them when they feel that you understand what you're talking about, and when they believe that your product is going to work for them. They will buy from you if you have these three things: They know you care about them. They know you know what you're talking about. They know that your product is going to work. Also, when you know your product is going to work, it's essential that you help your customers understand the benefits of the product.

For example, if you're talking to your customer about a car, they will want to know exactly what the benefits of the car are: whether it's better gas mileage with a hybrid, a bigger engine with a muscle car, or a higher lift to get off the ground when driving through the woods with a four-by-four. Are these good benefits? Is the four-by-four going to ensure that the family will have a great time? Is the muscle car going to make you feel like you've achieved that higher goal in life where you can purchase the vehicle that you want, not just your standard economy car? Does the hybrid, having better gas mileage and a more efficient battery, make you feel like you're giving back to the planet? That you're contributing by helping to save the world by reducing your carbon footprint.

These are some of the questions to ask when trying to make the sale. When we sell our customers, we want them to consider the lifetime value after they walk out of that car dealership with a specific product. Customers will sometimes respond with, "Wow, I've never thought about it like that before!" When you hear those words come out of their mouth, we understand that you have now become a trusted advisor to the customer and not just an average salesperson.

One particular tip we use when we're going up against our competitors is not to cut the price. Don't cut price and have a race to the bottom to see who can provide the lowest cost. Instead, raise the value. You can do many things to raise the value, such as bundling your specific product with other complimentary items. For instance, Tim sells a book. Instead of just selling the book, he sells the book plus a handy index card with the highlights and a training course along with it. This increases the value. Don't cut the price and instead try to raise the value.

One of the best pieces of advice that Tim gave was to think about the customer when thinking about increasing value. What's in it for the customer? What do they need to get to achieve success? This is a process of maturity in sales when we're not coming across as needy or desperate during the sales call. We're not trying to get customers to feel sorry for us in order to win the sale. Instead of thinking about our own bank account, we need to think about what's going to happen for the customer and the success that they're going to achieve through purchasing the product. Focus on how to ensure that your customer is going to win.

Another solid piece of advice that Tim told us is to work for the testimonials and not for the money. When you're working for the testimonials, you're going to be able to deliver everything you can possibly deliver to get your customers an even better result than what they already paid for. This can result in a positive customer testimonial for yourself and your business, which will help increase your sales.

We also have to remember that people do business with people they like. We should think of our customers as friends. How can we make our customers' lives better? When we think about this, the good deed will always be reciprocated. Sometimes, it becomes like a game. They'll do something good for you, and you'll want to do something even better for them. This may go back and forth, ensuring that all parties achieve exactly what they want.

Tim also suggested coming up with a New Year's revolution for friends, family, and customers. This is where you concentrate on helping others achieve their goals in life. When you focus on helping others, you can't help but be helped yourself.

When I asked Tim the question of what his most jaw-dropping sales story was, he told me that at the very beginning of his sales career, he used to charge people $35 for an hour-long session for hypnosis. If they bought two sessions, it would be $60. He was twenty-five-years old, and that's what he thought it was worth. He was making some money, but not much. Tim wondered how he was going to be able to pay his rent every month. Finally, he gathered up the courage to increase the price to $60 for a session. He wasn't sure who would actually want to pay $60 for a session, but when he went to a business coach, they said, "You've got to increase your prices. Do you think your sessions are more valuable? Yes, they definitely are. So increase the price to $200 a session."

However, Tim decided to stay at his original price for a number of years because his internal self-belief was that nobody was going to pay more than $100 for a session.

Then he met with another business coach who challenged Tim by suggesting, "You have to bundle your services. Come up with a mid-range package that lasts longer rather than just selling single sessions." Tim came up with a package that was $2,777. When he pitched this product to the first person, they asked if he'd take a check. Tim learned that his service was valued at that higher price point. Many people were willing to pay that amount of money for the service because they understood what it was worth.

There will always be around 20% of people who want something that's really cream-of-the-crop and the best product that you have to offer. Always make sure in your business that you have something that is super-high-dollar, super-high-value for those customers who want more. Don't devalue yourself like Tim initially did. Understand what your own value is, and be confident that you can deliver it at that price point.

Tim tells us that the more you charge your clients, the better results they will get. Work on hitting your customer's monetary threshold, whether that's $5,000, $50,000, or $500,000. Another tactic you can implement is applying what's called the takeaway method. This is pushing away the offer from your customer to give you money, ensuring that your customer is really ready to start the program. You push away the credit card or check and say, "I just want to make sure that you're ready to start this program." If they convince you that it's the right time for them, then you know they'll be on board. These are the two things you can do to guarantee that your customers will have success.

Tim has a system to ensure customers have the right beliefs. You need to have the right support, and they need to have the right system for success. Tim gave us his seven-step, multi-million-dollar sales formula. This is called the sales superstar checklist. The first step is to find the customer's pain. Most people want to move away from pain rather than move toward pleasure. Alternatively, we find that entrepreneurs often want to move toward pleasure rather than away from pain. For instance, most people who happen to find a random $100 would rather save it than spend it or invest it. You need to find out what their real pain is in order to be able to help them.

Step number two involves turning up the heat. Tim's example is, if you take a frog and you put it in a cold frying pan, and then turn up the hot burner; as the heat increases little by little, the frog will actually sit and cook in its own juices. But if you put a frog in a hot frying pan right away, it will jump right out. What he means with this example is that we need to ask questions that make the customer realize that without taking action now, it's going to result in more pain than they were already in before. Don't let your customers sit in a bad situation.

A long time ago, a salesman was talking to a Tim and was looking to help him make more money in his business. The salesman said, "How much money do you think you're leaving on the table every month?" Tim told him about $15,000. The salesman politely replied, "Well, $15,000 a month times 12 months is over 6 figures. Our program costs less than $15,000." This is an example of creating a no-brainer decision.

Number three on the checklist is to define the benefits of the solution. It's important that our customers look at our solution as an asset, not an expense. When our customers ask, "What's the result I will get after this program?" They're thinking of it as an expense rather than an asset. If our customers think of us as an asset, they are more engaged with us. And when they are more engaged, they will take action and receive the benefits of the solution they actually desire. You want to be seen as an asset and investment to the customer. Teach your customers what they already know, but also teach them something that they don't know during the sales conversation to become an asset.

Number four is to give the customer social proof. For example, Tim has a big paper binder of customer testimonials. He would hand the binder to customers and encourage them to read the testimonials, so they were convinced that his strategy worked. He provided them with social proof. We have to connect with the customer in a way that they'll respond to, whether that be through physical testimonials on paper, something online, an image, or a video platform.

Number five is we have to ask for the sale. In 70% of sales people do not ask for the sale. When you're asking for the sale, be confident. When a customer sees confidence in a salesperson, it helps them feel certain when they're making a decision.

Number six is to take away the risk. We find that a lot of programs out there have some sort of a guarantee, a 14-day guarantee, 30-day guarantee, etc. Let's use the modern gargantuan example of Amazon. We all know that if we buy something from Amazon and it isn't to our liking, we can return it in 30 days with no questions asked. They guarantee that if we're not satisfied with the products that come to our door, we can return them if we don't like them. We have no problem purchasing from Amazon.

Number seven is the penalty for not taking action. This is something that we want to offer to the customer by saying, "If you take action today, you'll get bonuses X, Y, and Z," or "By taking action today you'll be able to save 20% off your total sale." You could also say, "For the first few people that take advantage of this offer, you'll get something special in the mail." Be careful with this because your penalty for not taking action has to be truthful and credible. If you offer something a day after it expires or you bend the rules, then you lose all credibility.

If you look at business from a positive angle, there is no failure. There's only feedback from your customers. It can also be said that there are winners and there are learners. Instead of losing or failing, you're receiving the feedback and you're learning. You're learning from your mistakes and growing. On this notion, one of the questions that often comes up in business is about refunds.

There are two ways of approaching refunds. One, you have a clear policy that there are no refunds, no questions asked. Two, you can be a little bit more compassionate with your customers within reason. Even if you do have a no-refund policy, if you meant to give them results but they didn't actually achieve anything from your service; you can be surprised at what happens when you're compassionate.

Tim had one customer he charged $3,500, but they weren't showing up for the training sessions or doing any of the work. He also had a no-refunds stipulation in their contract. Tim told the customer, "Since we weren't able to get you any results, I'm just going to go ahead and refund you your $3,500," and they were shocked. They said, "That sounds great, but no refunds are written into the contract." Tim replied, "Well, I lost a little bit of time, but you didn't get your results. So we're going to give you back your money." What was awesome was that because he did this, the customer sent him three referrals that year for a total of $7,500 in additional sales. And when you get referral customers, those are always going to be the easiest customers to work with. They will receive the most benefit from your service.

Tim's actionable advice is to love yourself. Honor yourself and focus on who you are. Whatever you place your attention on will naturally expand in your life. What you think about yourself is who you'll become. Focus on the outcomes you want. As human beings, it's normal for us to focus on what we don't have or what we're lacking in life.

Tim explains that when you start moving rapidly toward your goals, your goals will start rapidly moving toward you. He said the hardest sale is selling yourself. You have to sell yourself on the belief that you can be and always do better. We're hardwired to be very comfortable with whoever we have become, living in the certain place that we're living, our economic status, our relationships, etc. But you need to sell yourself to be more valuable, which is where a mentor can come into play. Someone who can see that you are greater than maybe what you have already become.

Tim leaves us with this: "At the very end, you become more valuable to this world when you bring more value to yourself. Keep going, keep pushing forward, and be the best person that you can be."

To connect more with Tim Shurr, please visit:
https://timshurr.com

TRANSFERRING EMOTION

Troy Aberle and Luke Aberle

Troy Aberle is a business acceleration master, entrepreneur, best-selling author, and philanthropist. He is a recognized authority on the psychology of leadership, negotiations, and organizational turnaround, and has served as an advisor to many leaders in business.

Luke Aberle earns the spot of being a very unique 11-year-old entrepreneur. He started his career at 8 years old when he developed a deep passion to learn more about batteries and camping gear.

I met Troy and Luke Aberle at a conference called OfferMind in Boise, Idaho. I flew to Idaho a few days before the event, knowing there were several people I was very interested to meet in person. People like Kevin Stevens and Kathy Walls. I went to lunch one day at P.F. Chang's with Troy and Luke as well as several others who were there for the conference. I had already eaten a large breakfast at the hotel, so I wasn't hungry, but I knew that being at the right place and growing my relationships was beneficial. Troy and Luke caught my attention because of their caring nature and genuine personalities.

I was sitting at the opposite end of the table from them and toward the end of the lunch, I walked over to their side to introduce myself. The first thing that hit me was how impressed I was with Luke Aberle. He carried himself extremely maturely despite being only eleven years old. This young man spoke as if he were twenty years older (and was even more mature than some thirty-year-old people I know). Luke told me about what he was doing with his YouTube channel, Luke's View. Luke reviews outdoor products, giving a kid's opinion in an adult world.

As we all walked to the next location, I also had a conversation with Troy, who asked me what I was doing in business. I told him that my profession was in sales. Troy is a coach and has worked with a number of entrepreneurs, as well as sales professionals. Some of these are large companies like John Deere. We talked about what sales meant to each other and how we had the best interest of the customer in mind. Most salespeople are only interested in filling their own wallets with cash, but he was not like that. I respected this highly, and we decided to exchange phone numbers so we could connect in the future. Because of this connection, Troy ended up working with me on this virtual summit. Troy got me in touch with a number of individuals on the summit, and I'm very thankful for this relationship. He was also one of the people who challenged me to put this event together.

For Luke and Troy, sales is simply the transfer of emotion. This the number one thing people should know about, not just in sales, but life in general. It's the transfer of emotion from the product to the customer, and also the money from the customer moving toward yourself. Tony Robbins, a life coach, teaches that people purchase to gain pleasure or to move away from pain. For instance, if you're driving down the Pacific Coast Highway in Santa Monica, California, and you want the wind blowing in your hair and a date with you, you're moving toward pleasure. When Luke reviews physical products, he is letting customers know exactly which products to buy and which ones not to buy. This way people can potentially move toward a place they need to be or away from the pain they're already in.

To be effective in sales, simply add more value to your customers than your competitors do. It forces you through the process of matching up a need from the customer with a product or service you have. For them to purchase, the customer does need to be satisfied with your product. According to Troy, sales is the best when somebody gives him a referral. And there's a reason for this. Not only does it make you feel good as a salesperson, but when customers give you a referral, they remember how awesome it was to do business with you and how much they enjoyed the product. The customer actually wants to share that positive experience with others.

Troy and Luke talked of the six human needs and how they apply to sales for your customers. The first one is certainty. Customers need to have certainty that they're going to get the service or the products they desire. For example, McDonald's is all over this world although it's widely known that these burgers and fries are not as healthy as something that was grass fed or organic. But because we all know what that McDonald's hamburger tastes like, and we're familiar with it, we are certain of the outcome. That's the reason why people eat at this restaurant.

The second is variety or uncertainty. If you're buying a tripod and are looking into the competition, the competition can't just be another tripod that's a buck cheaper. There has to be value that's different than your competition to have that variety or uncertainty.

The third one is the need to feel significant. Customers always want to feel like they're a rock star, and they want to feel that they've been able to do something good. If a portion of your proceeds goes to cleaning up our oceans, recycling plastic, or planting a tree, it will help customers feel significant.

The fourth is love, connection, and relationships. These are important because we want our customers to know that we care about them. They should know that we care about them more than just our own wallets.

The fifth is the need for growth. Simply said, If you aren't growing, you're dying. And nobody ever wants to deal with a salesperson who is not growing or is negative. For instance, you always want to be able to tell your customers something positive that's happening in life. It doesn't have to be that you won the World Cup, or you just gave birth to a child. It can be something as simple as telling them that the flowers you planted in your backyard are starting to bloom. Customers want to hear something that's positive, and they want to hear about growth.

The last one is contribution. As human beings, we love to be able to contribute to someone or something else. For example, if we go into a coaching program and ask our customers to contribute to our cause after we've been able to help them achieve their desired result, you'll be surprised at the number of customers who are genuinely interested in giving back after they've seen success.

Luke and Troy provided an example of using some of the human needs with a specific product. They received a knife from Cold Steel, and it had a unique shape. The product gives certainty to the customer that they have a high-quality product. It gives uncertainty and variety being that this knife is uniquely shaped. It is not like every other knife that's out there for hunting or camping. You feel significant because you're going to be able to prepare for the wild on your hunting or camping excursion. Because of this product, you'll be looked up to as someone who can provide protection. That'll translate into love, connection, and relationships as you'll be able to communicate with others and grow your relationships.

Luke also experienced growth because he's going to be the first eleven-year-old boy to review a product like this on the YouTube platform. He's able to give back to Cold Steel just as they gave him the product.

Once, Troy sold a six-figure John Deere tractor to a customer. The customer told him that he was going to buy the tractor from him, even though his price was $40,000 greater than his competition. The reason why was because the customer trusted that Troy was going to support him if anything went wrong. Troy's company was different because they were giving back to Air Rescue. The customer knew the quality was there with that specific product. He had never owned a John Deere tractor and always wanted to. He believed the tractor would do what it was meant to do. In buying that product from Troy, he knew Troy was going to support him. The customer was also going to have the growth that he needed in his business. And what Troy displayed was hitting those six human needs with that specific customer to get that huge sale.

When we think about sales in general, there are three questions that we should always ask ourselves: What is my customer's problem? What's the promise that I'm going to deliver to my customer? What process am I going to take the customer through to ensure that I deliver my promise? Problem, promise, and process. Without those three things, it is very hard to hit the six human needs and is close to impossible to sell any product. When you deliver on these three aspects, it's about you being honest with your customer. This results in going home with integrity when selling. One of the hardest things that we're ever going to have in sales is to go home and wonder if our customer believed us or not. This is why we want to hit on the problem, the promise, and the process.

Troy and Luke left us with a few pieces of actionable advice. The first piece is to ask for referrals. When you serve your customer well and you have a great product, some of the best and easiest sales and leads you'll find will come from referrals. So simply asking your customer, "Do you like my product/service? Can you recommend a buddy or two that I could contact, or would you be willing to pass this information along?" When customers have a positive experience with you, they will be more than happy to give you a referral.

Another one is to get very clear on exactly who your ideal customer is. You have to talk to the right customer for your message to resonate with them. When you speak their language, when they feel like you're talking directly to them and not to somebody in general, their ears perk up and they listen.

Finally, you've got to follow through with sales. Each salesperson needs to ask if there is anything additional that is needed from the customer after the product is sold. And this is going to do a few things. First, it'll validate your success in sales and the success of your product. Second, if there's anything that's missing, you'll be able to fill in those gaps to ensure that you get a good testimonial at the end and to also get a referral.

Troy gave us one piece of golden information. He said there are three fears we have as salespeople. The first is the fear of failure, which is obvious because if we don't get the sale then we don't make any money. The second is the fear of success. Salespeople actually fear that they will be successful because, not only do they have to deliver their product, but they're going to make more money, so they'll have more work to do with taxes, etc. The last is the fear of self-worthiness. Salespeople always think to themselves, *Who am I to sell this product? Am I really worth a customer paying this kind of money?*

When I asked Luke what his most difficult sale was, he told me that it was getting companies that have outdoor products to trust an eleven-year-old young man to review their products. You might be thinking, *Who wouldn't give an eleven-year-old an opportunity to review a product?* But in reality, the business world can be tough. So he works very hard at it, which is why his YouTube channel and product reviews are so successful.

Troy's most difficult sale was during one specific sale to a company that had purchased millions of dollars-worth of farm equipment before. Troy was selling them another tractor and assumed the sale since they had already done a lot of business. His customer told Troy that he actually lost the sale to an auction house of all places. He was shocked. He didn't think something like that would happen and had no idea why they would go to an auction house. Troy asked his customer why they did it and was told that they didn't feel Troy had their best interests in mind. They didn't feel that he was going to support his product. And for those reasons, they went elsewhere to go try to find a deal.

That company was going to continue to buy from auction houses because they were able to get the product, and it was a fast and easy transaction. This bothered Troy quite a bit, so he thought about things for a while. He then went back to his customer and said, "I own up to it. I am sorry. I wasn't thinking about your best interests. And I would really like to support you in the future. What can I do to make this right?" By owning up to his mistake of not caring for his customer and following through, he was eventually able to win back the customer and regain the business. This teaches us that we must always keep the customer's best interests in mind. Keeping the customer first is absolutely vital day in and day out, even if we have customers who are repeat buyers.

To connect more with Troy Aberle, please visit:
https://www.troyaberle.com

To connect more with Luke Aberle, please visit:
www.lukesview.com

RETURN ON RELATIONSHIP

Christopher Vos

Christopher is an entrepreneur and founder of The ROR Method. He helps people looking to connect with their dream clients and get noticed by influencers in their fields.

Troy Aberle introduced me to Christopher Vos. One evening I was on a Zoom call with Troy and he said, "You know what? Let's get a hold of Christopher Vos because I know he has a huge impact with sales. You will want to interview him for your virtual event and book" This was about nine o'clock in the evening. Fortunately, we were able to connect with Christopher over a web call while he was working out on the treadmill.

Christopher Vos is amazing. He is a proud father of *nine* children, works out every single day, and has an awesome work ethic. Christopher and Troy have such a fantastic relationship, so Christopher was nice enough to talk to us during his workout, and I had the honor of interviewing him. He is the founder of the ROR Method, which stands for "return on relationship." He's been using this specific sales method since he was a child.

Christopher teaches us that sales is about relationships, pure and simple. People don't care about how much you know until they know how much you care. In sales, which is about far more than just money, your net worth is equal to your network. Without a doubt, the growth of sales is directly related to the relationships you have, and these relationships have to be authentic. You have to care about more than just yourself. You need to care about the people you serve.

The reason why Christopher is so passionate about the ROR method is because he is alive today and contributing to this book because of this method. In July of 2019, he had a stroke. He was previously put through a health, wellness, and fitness program with an individual he had a good relationship with. Because of that return on relationship, he was physically fit enough to get through the stroke, be healthy, and not pass away. He's thankful to be alive today because of that particular reason.

Through helping individuals, Christopher noticed that people naturally ask you how they can provide a return on your relationship. For instance, think about what it would be like if you went to see your dream customer and instead of you asking for their business, they asked how they could help *you*? When you do things for other people, and you're able to benefit and impact their life, they will likely ask what they can do for you in return.

Once, Christopher was on the phone with someone who decided his assignment the next day was to call Christopher to figure out what he could do to positively impact Christopher's life or his business. This gentleman wouldn't take no for an answer. This return on relationship has been the driving force behind his business and life. The ROR method took his business from nobody knowing who he was to becoming a well-known name in the industry. I know it's cliché, but you want to dig your well *before* you're thirsty. Establish relationships at the very beginning.

One of the key aspects of the ROR method is how to get noticed in a sea of other competitors. There is a movie called *Hitch* where Will Smith plays a character named Alex Hitchens. Albert Brennaman is another character in the movie, an overweight and pretty average guy who's trying to get noticed by a beautiful model; who Alex Hitchens helps. It's a good example of the ROR method because Alex is helping Albert get noticed in a large sea of other competitors fighting for the model's attention.

When you're trying to get the attention of somebody who is well-known or famous in your industry, whether it be Michael Jordan, Kevin Harrington, Mark Cuban, Alicia Keys, or any other celebrity; you need to do something that will help you stand above the competition. For example, Christopher helped me out with working on getting connected with an individual from the Ziglar family. He keyed in on a specific factor that I naturally overlooked. This family member had a very strong involvement with the Christian faith. Christopher said it would be good if I gave the individual a small gift of gratitude. He helped me design a chest with a Bible in it, as well as a phrase from Nehemiah 8:10, which is *For the joy of the Lord is my strength*. I sent this to the individual while utilizing the ROR method to get noticed in a sea of other competitors.

You have to genuinely care about the other person. When I gave the gift, it showed that I also cared about my own Christian faith. In the movie *Hitch*, Brennaman authentically cared about the attractive model and wanted to get to know her. There was another guy who was trying to consult with Alex Hitchens on how to sleep with a girl, but he had only selfish intent in mind. This was figuring out how to get his physical needs met. He didn't care about the feelings of the woman he was trying to hook up with. This shows us that using the ROR method authentically works but using it selfishly does not.

Christopher told me a story about when his grandfather was in the hospital. He passed away at 102 years old, which was a celebration of life. Christopher was explaining to his grandfather exactly what the ROR method was. His grandfather said, "You know what? This is how I've been doing business my whole life. This is the old way of doing business, and it is tried and true. People buy from people that they know and like."

I have a story of my own I'd like to share. There was someone who I had been trying to get into business with for a long time. He had some major accounts, and I decided I wanted to pitch to him. I tried everything under the sun. From attempting to take him out to lunch, emailing him, telling him all about the features and benefits of what I was selling; nothing grabbed his attention. I knew my product would help his customers. I brought in donuts. I did presentations. I sent him a slideshow. I even did multiple follow-up phone calls, but again none of it worked. Until one summer when I caught a bunch of bluefin tuna. I gave away the tuna to friends, cooked some for family, and had leftovers. I chose to pack an ice chest full of tuna and take it out to the Central Valley in California because I wanted to do something a bit more personal for him. I wasn't giving tuna to him and hoping he would give me business. I didn't really think anything of it. I didn't have any sort of ulterior motive other than wanting to do something kind.

So this individual, who ignored my phone calls and wouldn't give me the time of day, all of a sudden was willing to see me. I gave him this bag of fish and the response I got was amazing. He opened wide up, and we went on to do a lot of business together. We actually became friends and still are to this day. He invited me over for dinner to see his dogs and to meet his wife, who's a wonderful cook. The ROR method won't work until you're very authentic about getting to know somebody.

If you want to get somebody something that will make a difference, make sure there's a personal aspect to it. This shows that you did a little bit of research and took time out of your day. For myself, I took the time and the money to go fishing, I took the time to prepare the tuna, the time to bag it up nicely, and then effort to drive it all the way out to the Central Valley. And those are the things that really matter. There's a simple survey called *You Dig Your Wealth* that makes you think about people and what's really important to them because it's about them. It's not about you.

Christopher has two pieces of actionable advice for us. He insists that one of the most important things we can do for ourselves at the beginning of every single day is to change our state of mind and how we think about things. To do this, let's look at how to apply this advice in two ways.

The first one is to go on Amazon or to the drugstore and buy a pack of thank-you cards. Every morning, write a thank-you card to someone to tell them you're thankful for what they've been able to teach you. You're thankful for being able to serve them in business. You're thankful for some connection that they were able to make for you or whatever it may be. This is going to change the way you do business as well as change the way that you subconsciously are selling.

Next, send two text messages every day and thank someone for what they did. This approach is very similar to doing thank-you cards, and again, will get you in a state of gratitude. By thinking of others and being grateful, you'll dig your well, build your relationships, and plant those seeds. I guarantee you will see a positive change in your business.

There's nothing wrong with thinking about yourself and your business, but I want you to remember that you need to dig your well *before* you're thirsty. This is because in sales, we're always going to get thirsty. If you don't have anywhere to go, you'll be on a long road, which can be extremely dry, difficult, and potentially sales empty. Build your relationships so when you are in need, you'll have a helping hand to reach out to.

Christopher's most difficult sale was convincing his wife to have nine kids with him. He said you need to build a sturdy foundation and implement the ROR method. This allows you to understand that you're giving just as much as you're receiving. Again, it's that core base that you're able to build on top of.

I'll wrap up with the importance of playing long-term and building a foundation. According to Christopher, whether it was from our founding fathers or guys like Thomas Edison, everybody back then was thinking long-term. They knew it was going to take time to achieve their goals, which is how you'll get success that lives on well into the future. Burnout is inevitable in business, and you can't hustle forever. Christopher explains that, when you play the short game, you'll experience failures that will make it very easy to give up. You can get a quick win, but also lose just as fast. When you play the long game, make sure to have the end in mind and reach for that lifelong goal.

To connect more with Christopher Vos, please visit:
http://www.therormethod.com

BEING TRUTHFUL TO CUSTOMERS AND YOURSELF

Jim Padilla and Cyndi Padilla

Jim is a master sales trainer, an expert team builder, and a launch expert. With more than twenty years of experience building teams and leading them to success, Jim has a solid track record of achieving results.

Cyndi is a master team builder and motivator. After a successful career in retail store leadership, she turned her attention to her passion—developing teams.

I met Jim Padilla through a ClickFunnels Facebook group. I reached out to see who some of the sales experts inside of the group were, and Jim's name came up multiple times. We had a very short chat where he told me that he was in business with his wife, Cyndi Padilla, and that he does most of his business merely through referrals. He also does a lot of speaking engagements and digital platforms, such as virtual summits and podcasting. It was only natural that I wanted to know how he built up his sales business.

First, let me tell you how Jim and Cyndi met. Jim was on the entrepreneur journey, and six years ago, Cyndi decided she was going to give up her 9-5 employee life in retail management and work with her husband as entrepreneurs. She didn't want to be in the retail world anymore and was not going to go through another retail Black Friday. There aren't too many husband and wife teams that are able to do business together, but Jim and Cyndi are rock stars in sales, and they make it happen every day.

They both have a very unique perspective on sales. Jim says that sales is the most essential skill set in life. People process sales every single day. They're naturally selling without even being aware they're doing so. Whether you feel like you need to be a professional in sales or sales is the most important thing to you in your business, you're naturally doing sales every day.

Cyndi tells us sales is not about what you do or say during the sale. It isn't about how you prepare and think about your pitch. Sales is truly just who you are and how you're trying to impact people in a positive way. Sales is being a leader. Instead of it being you against the customer, think about trying to lead your customer in the right direction, down the correct path, and to that personal decision—as long as it will be beneficial for them.

Jim's sales story is very powerful. He was born to teenage parents, and his father ended up leaving. Jim was on the streets at sixteen and was frequently exposed to violence. Around the age of nineteen, he ended up in jail. He understood that sales was truly about influencing the people around him to do the right things. When he was on the streets, he tried to influence people around him that he was the good guy, He sold that he was on their side, so they wouldn't hurt him.

Cyndi has a very interesting story as well. Once, she was having a sales conversation with a woman who had just purchased a $30,000 program. The next step in the process for her was to invest in a $45,000 program. Her customer was ready to invest quickly. Cyndi said to herself, *Wow, so this person is just going to invest $75,000 in a very short period.* Cyndi knew she wasn't prepared for the pitch, and as a result, she dropped the offer to the customer and wasn't able to close the sale. Cyndi took a hard look at herself and saw exactly how she wasn't prepared. She called the customer back and said, "You know, I was ill-prepared. I want to own up to this. I wasn't ready for this conversation. This is exactly what the offer looks like, and this is why it's going to benefit you…" and then she was able to close the sale.

What we learned from this is that there's a lot of power in just being truthful and honest during your sales presentations. You can think about sales in two different ways. One is you can be the most prepared: know every nuance about your product and customer, do all the research you can in the beginning, and come to the presentation like a rock star.

Or, you can be the most connected to who you are as a person, who you are serving, and exactly what that conversation looks like. This is more of a subconscious method of selling, which is just talking to people, having a conversation, not feeling the pressure of the words *sales* or *sales calls*. It's almost impossible to say the wrong thing with this system. More often than not, you find yourself consistently always attracting the right customer and saying the right things without even thinking about it. In this methodology, you definitely know who you are, what you want your customers to do, and exactly how you need to show up to the conversation every single time.

Take some time and dive into those two different components. Be the most prepared and know every nuance about your product and customer. These include specific elements like having the proper follow-up, understanding your marketing emails, and nurturing your lead after you've been able to get their opt-in or get them on the phone. It's about having the right pre-frame during your sales funnel, driving them to an educational webinar, having your customers purchase one of your free books, or just being on time for your call and showing up. It's those specific details that will matter the most for you to be fully prepared.

On the other hand, when we're taking a look at being the most connected to who you are and who you're serving; that's more the subconscious way of having that sales conversation. Jim tells us this is almost like the 'park bench approach.' If you were at a park, sitting on a bench with somebody for 30 minutes, you should be able to know exactly who they are, what they desire to have in life, and what kind of path they need to be on to go get it. This is your more natural conversation and is very, very important. Whether you're meeting somebody over the web, in person, or on the phone, you should know within thirty minutes how to get them from where they are to their desired location. The goal for these two pieces is for you to be a communications facilitator and a solution provider.

I asked Jim about his hardest sale outside of his business. Cyndi laughed because one of the hardest sales he had was getting her to marry him. He had actually proposed to her three times before she said yes. But when he thought about it a little more, one of the most difficult sales he had was to win back his children. Back in 2008 and 2009, when we were in financial hard times here in America, Jim was doing business in real estate. He was trying to invest his money properly but wasn't able to get the return on investment that some advisors had promised. He didn't tell Cyndi what he was doing with the money since he figured he'd invest it, make it back, and it would fly under the radar so low that Cyndi wouldn't even notice. They didn't even have a joint bank account, so he figured it wasn't a big deal.

When it came time to recapture some of those funds, they weren't there. Jim meant to tell Cyndi that they were in a lot of debt and that he had no idea how to pay it off. When he finally did tell her what was going on, she was pretty upset. Not that they were in debt, but because Jim hid the information from her. It strained their relationship, and they separated for about a year and a half. At that time, they had three kids, and their oldest didn't talk to Jim for six years. Their middle child didn't talk to him for three years. The youngest was a daddy's girl, so she stuck around.

Jim's hardest sale was to get his daughters to speak to him again. One day he received a handwritten letter from one of his daughters telling him that they didn't even know how he got into the situation with the money, but they loved him. During dinner one night, one of them asked Jim to officiate her and her fiancé's marriage.

One of the hardest sales Cyndi had also was with their daughter. She wanted to sell them on becoming the best person they could be and to continually grow in life. One of their daughters was still living at home at eighteen and was engaging in behavior that was unhealthy for the family. It was a tough decision, but Jim and Cyndi had to kick their daughter out of the house. Fortunately, their daughter realized she was in the wrong. She came back three weeks later and apologized by bringing Cyndi flowers, and then succeeded on the road of going to college, getting a job, etc. Despite it being difficult, it is always extremely rewarding to be able to sell to your kids.

To connect more with Jim and Cyndi Padilla, please visit:
https://salesunscripted.com

STRATEGIES AND SYSTEMS

To be successful in selling, you need to implement specific strategies and systems. The gift of gab will not get you to the top of the leaderboard nor will going through an unplanned hustle routine. One sale I will never forget was the $218,000 sale I won at MillerCoors.

This was a sale I prepared for and executed over a number of value-based sales calls. The sale ended up taking well over six months to win, but the plan was executed in several mini-steps and victories. Since day one, our team needed to control the situation from every point from the security guard to the lead director, who would make the final decision. Without this control, you always run the risk of competitors stealing away your business and customers getting lost in the purchasing decision. A confused customer never buys.

One extremely important part that influenced the win was storytelling. I needed to sell both the product and myself. We were pitching a canning solution for CoorsLite and Pabst Blue Ribbon. I got our team together and told MillerCoors a similar success story of a job that we had done at Samuel Adams. We had saved Sam Adams well over $100,000 in production costs and also increased their production rate, vastly increasing their profits.

Even though I had given them a great case study, I still had to tell one more story. It was my turn to tell MillerCoors a story of myself. People do business with people, so it was my turn to step up to the plate. We were up against a competitor whose product was a fraction of our price, so I chose to tell a story of how I was not in it for the money. Years ago, The Tropicana hotel and casino in Las Vegas was experiencing high energy usage. We had a heating and cooling solution which was four times my competitors' price. Despite this, I had the best interest of the customer in mind, and I sold them the solution. The end result was a cost-saving on energy and product longevity. This story helped to prove my credibility and trust with the customer.

High-dollar project sales often have complex sales structures. It is important for us to remember our sales system and to relate our personal and professional stories to win these deals. The upcoming chapters will give you expert insight on how to successfully do this.

RESULTS BY PREPARATION AND PERFECTION

Eric Lofholm

Eric Lofholm is a master sales trainer who has taught his proven sales systems to thousands of professionals around the world. He is president and CEO of Eric Lofholm International, Inc., an organization he founded to professionally train people on the art and science of selling.

Seth Greene (from the SharkPreneur podcast with Kevin Harrington) introduced me to Eric Lofholm. Seth initially sent me an email which said Eric had helped Kevin with his launch of the book and course, *Secrets of Closing the Sale,* with Kevin Harrington and Zig Ziglar. He told me that Eric was a great person to be connected to for sales, and he thought we should have a chat. Eric and I talked about the end goal for the Ultimate Sales Momentum and we found a mutually beneficial fit.

Eric tells us that sales equals service. You should sell from a place of honesty, integrity, and compassion. Selling is about leading and moving people to action. When we think of sales as more than just money, we understand that selling is a style of communication to increase the likelihood of another person saying yes. It is an empowering skill set to get the life that you desire.

Eric is all about teaching and sharing professional knowledge with others. Earlier in his career, he ended up in San Diego, California and wanted to work for the ultimate business coach, Tony Robbins, so he went and applied for a job. He was granted an interview, but it didn't work out. Eric started to think about who he knew that was in the same network as Tony Robbins. He asked one of his acquaintances if he could potentially be pointed in the right direction to an individual Tony worked with. That individual got contacted, then Eric was asked to come in for another interview. He got the job soon after.

The funny thing is he got this job just about two weeks after his previous denial. Eric ultimately created his own referral and opened a door into the company. This was a huge win for him because he stayed there for about three years and was able to springboard his success for his own business. We learn from Eric's story that when you decide you want something, you should definitely go for it. He didn't even hear the rejections. He just knew he was going to go work for Tony Robbins.

Eric talked about his sales methodology which is a simply three steps: the sales model, the sales mountain, and the sales script. The sales model is how many times you meet with the prospect before they decide to buy from you. For example, when Girl Scouts are selling cookies outside of the grocery store, it's considered a one-call close because they don't ask you for a business card. They don't want to follow up. They're going to sell you a box of cookies, and you're going to buy one.

The sales mountain is the call outline for each time you meet with the prospect. Ask yourself what are the key points that you need to cover and what order to cover them in. It is very important to outline each of these steps before the sales call.

The third part is the sales script. Outline each point of the sales mountain with its own mini-script. This means you have a certain order and set of talking points that you need to take your customer through to win the sale. When you go through these three steps—the sales model, sales mountain, and sales script—it intensifies the persuasiveness of the presentation and also increases your closing ratio.

Eric gave an excellent example of how this process works. As an example, let's take a band that goes on tour.

They have twelve songs they play during each concert. After the twelve songs, the crowd yells for an encore and then the band comes back out. They play their last two great songs. This band knows that if they go to Los Angeles, California, and they play these twelve songs in a specific order, the crowd will always yell for an encore. The band will come back out, play the last two songs, get a standing ovation, and have a successful tour. This process can be repeated throughout Phoenix, Arizona; Washington, DC; Dallas, Texas; Orlando, Florida; and so on. The methodology can be used time and time again, just like your sales presentation. Once you've proven this methodology, this is your license to print money through sales.

Eric pointed out that humans naturally resist sales. We don't want to appear "salesy," so many salespeople will be unprepared and unscripted because they don't want to be *that scripted predictable* person. This is not the right way to perform sales. You need to come in prepared for the sales call. When you do, you have the ability to find out what part of your sales process needs to be improved upon when you have that certain system in place. Then when you perfect the process and you perfect the system, you can repeat it for success.

For predictable results, there are two choices: you can either go into the sales presentation prepared or unprepared. The question is, what will give the customer more value? What will make the customer feel that you have more confidence? The answer is, of course, being prepared. The methodology is so simple, but it is not digested by most salespeople. This sales methodology has to be put into action to be successful. The best thing is when it generates success for you, it can do the same for your entire team as well.

Eric has two pieces of actionable advice. One is to always be prospecting. The thing that drives the sales engine is prospecting. If you ask a room full of salespeople if they think they should be doing more prospecting, they'll all answer yes. Also, if you gamify your prospecting, your sales results will naturally increase.

By gamifying your prospecting you need to reach out to a certain number of people every day, whether that's five, ten, twenty, etc. The more prospecting you do, the more sales you'll close. Just make sure you hit that number every single day. Don't think about the rejection, don't think about the wins, just count the number of prospects that you reach out to. If you have twenty-five people you need to reach out to every day, and you find out that for every five people you get one yes. Then out of those twenty-five you're going to close five sales. Those results become predictable at 20%. When you can increase those results and get more sales closes, you'll increase your bottom-line revenue.

The second piece of actionable advice is to take massive action. This comes in a four-step process. The first step is put in a full workweek. The second step is, during the workweek, be present and productive. The third step is to have a plan for each day on exactly what you want to accomplish. The fourth and final step is to ask yourself what you can do to be more productive every day. These are very simple suggestions, yet they are often neglected by salespeople and business individuals. But these will get you to increase results within your business, guaranteed. The reason why Eric is considered to be the continuous improvement sales guy is because he knows that your sales skills and results can always get better if you continue to work on them.

Eric told us about a well-known individual who was selling insurance policies. The man grew from a very novice, very beginner salesperson to the number one sales guy in the whole country. He always knew that he could sell three insurance policies a week. How could he go from being 'green' and the newest guy on the team to number one in the world by selling three policies a week? He became more effective and efficient with his time. He went through the four-step system by taking massive action.

Eric told me about an awesome sale he made outside of his current business. He initially had worked for Tony Robbins. Unfortunately, their accounting department one time calculated his paycheck incorrectly. They had overpaid him by $10,000, and because Eric's an honest man, he had every intention of giving the money back. But they were not able to fix this before his last day of work.

Not long after, they asked for their ten grand back. Eric said, "I can't give you ten grand because I had to pay the State of California tax. Some of it went to the 401k. I was able to net something a little over $5,000, so I'm not going to pay you ten grand." The Tony Robbins company said they were going to sue him, so Eric suggested they come up with some sort of agreement. He suggested he could work off the money with the company by doing sales coaching. He made $500 a day doing that, much earlier in his career.

Eric ended up paying off the ten grand and furthermore did a total of 18 months' worth of work at the Tony Robbins company, netting $40,000. This kickstarted his sales coaching business and career. It is an extreme example of turning a potential negative into the highest positive for himself and his business. One of the things we learn is this all stemmed from his honesty, integrity, and determination to barter with the company and work as a sales coach. This is a fantastic win-win experience. The icing on the cake is that Eric can always say that Tony Robbins hired him as a sales trainer, which puts a nice feather in his cap.

To connect with Eric Lofholm, please visit:
https://saleschampion.com

CONTROLLING YOUR ENVIRONMENT

Ace Reddy

Ace Reddy is an influencer, entrepreneur, and Facebook Ads Wizard. He has over 4,000 students from 120 countries and is one of the most respected Facebook Ad geniuses on the planet.

I was introduced to Ace Reddy through Kathy Walls. Kathy recommended Ace to me because he is an individual who has a great mindset about marketing skills and how they significantly impact sales.

Ace and I had a short conversation over the phone prior to our interview. He said that sales is about helping people get what they want but being able to collect money yourself during the process. Sales and making money are related. Also, helping people and making money is related. You need to stay motivated to help your customers get the results they want.

It's important to help people while also helping yourself. For example, If you don't have any money in the bank and are worried about how you can pay the bills. Then you won't be very successful at helping others. When we think about sales, we need to make sure there's a balance between the value you give your customers and what you get paid.

When you charge your customers, they're going to value your service or product based on what you charge. For instance, if you give somebody something for free, it is very unlikely they will value that product. But if you charge them a higher amount, they will attach value relative to the amount you charge. Make sure the value equals the service you provide—do not overcharge and do not undercharge. When you create this balance, you won't lose the motivation to run your own business (because you're not making enough money) and your customers will be happier with the results they receive.

Ace had an amazing sales story, which plays to the point where a lot of individuals will tell you that you just need to help people instead of selling them. But the two—sales and helping people—actually go hand in hand. Ace put his heart and effort into a very valuable webinar he ran for free back in 2018. Over ninety people attended his webinar, but he did not receive any testimonials. He didn't get any results for his attendees.

A little while later, he decided to charge $97 for the same webinar. He only sold thirty spots, but of those thirty, he received testimonials from his webinar. One of the testimonials was from someone who made a million dollars off of the information that was on his webinar. Another person was making over $300,000 a month. He then realized that there's a direct correlation between the money that you charge for your specific product and the actions and the results that not only your customers get, but that you receive as well.

Today's world is a world of consumerism. In the movie *Fight Club*, Brad Pitt's character, Tyler Durden, says that people buy stuff they don't even need. People want to buy stuff more than they want to be sold stuff. We need to keep offering products to people. Advertising and sales need to take place. Advertising takes up about 80% of that sale because you need to be able to get the product to the customer or make the customer aware of the product.

Ace explained there are three core questions we need to ask ourselves with advertising, which focus on the market and the customer: Who is buying? What are they buying? Who are they already buying from? When you're able to analyze these three questions, you'll be able to come up with a product and target the market correctly when selling your product. You want to make sure that your customers will buy your product before you spend hours and days creating it. To put it simply, look for problems customers have and sell them the solution.

Once you think you have the solution, you need to test your products until you find one that's a winner where the market responds to what you want to sell them. And if you don't get the validation from the market for your product or offer, you run the risk of your product not converting well. Put the time and effort into creating something, but only if you have first validated it with the market.

There's a lot of add-ons in sales that can help increase conversions like fancy marketing, a great logo, website, and much more. But if you don't know that your market is asking for the specific products you have and they're also willing to pay for it, then no fancy widget will save you.

Ace is an expert in advertising and gave us some valuable information about getting traffic. Organic traffic, attracting your market for free, is very hard. It's tough to grow a Facebook page or Instagram account to thousands of followers. But if you pay for the traffic, it's much simpler. Also, you can test the market with paid traffic and find out quickly what converts and what doesn't. It all comes down to if you have more time or more money.

Ace had a lot of great actionable advice; the first piece is for all of us to study the field. We need to understand what customers need and exactly what they're responding to. Study the field and see what kinds of courses and products are already out there. It will allow you to validate your own ideas. Read up on the material that's working, watch the webinars that are working, read the emails that are working, and model them.

Also, pick one mentor and learn from them by watching all their material. Conflict of information causes pain or discomfort in your mind, which happens when you have more than one mentor at the same time. When you have two mentors teaching you conflicting ideas, you will be confused. And when you're confused, you won't take action. Without taking action, you won't see results. And if you do decide to move from one mentor to another one, make sure you pick one who you connect with and then stay with them.

Look within your current mentor's inner circle or recommended people. That way the influential material you're getting will stay consistent, so long as it is working inside of your business. It doesn't matter what you do as long as you do it with quantity and quality. With mentors and coaching, the good ones will work as long as you go all in.

Learn from a mentor for sixty days. If you see improvement, then continue. But if you don't see improvement, drop them and unlearn all the information that you've been taught. This isn't something you want to try to force to work just because you spent time and money. Think of it as an investment and move forward.

Ace also discussed being mindful of the advice you receive from family members or friends. Use your business mentor to filter this advice. Our families and friends usually have our best interests in mind, but if their advice conflicts with what our mentors are teaching us, it'll create a confused mindset. Use your mentors as that filter for the advice from them.

It's very important to get everybody you're talking to inside of your circle on the same page. When that happens and you're hearing the same things, you should start seeing progress. There's a saying that you become like the people you surround yourself with. If you surround yourself with like-minded people who are successful in a very similar way, you will become successful as well.

Ace shared that the most difficult sale he had to overcome outside of his business had to do with controlling his environment. These were the people who surround him: family, friends, co-workers, etc. If you listen to information long enough, especially if it's coming from the people closest to you, you will end up believing it. Subconsciously, when we hear things, we digest the information (or opinions) as facts. It's very important we control the people we're around as well as the situations we put ourselves into.

Ace tells us a story about this. He is six feet four inches tall and was 260 pounds at one point. He worked with a weight loss specialist who taught him how to count calories. In the beginning, he lost four pounds a week. Then he was consistently losing two pounds a week, week after week. He ended up doing this for about a year and lost around 90 pounds.

One day, somebody told him that counting calories didn't work and that he would be better off going with another diet like Keto or Atkins. He listened and hung around this individual for a long time. The result was that Ace had stopped losing weight because he stopped counting calories. He had doubts in his mind and was no longer getting any weight loss results. This is a good example of how you have to be extremely careful of the people you surround yourself with because they can subconsciously influence your actions and results, whether you know it's happening or not. The good news is Ace is back on track now.

When you pick a mentor and decide who you'll associate with, make sure they are all people who are headed in the right direction. When you pick a mentor, pick one who has gone through everything and has seen what does and doesn't work. That way, you can see exactly what their path looks like and decide if it's one you want to follow and go all in with.

The last piece of advice from Ace is that doubt is the main killer of all dreams and sales. This is true in your business or your personal life. Doubt occurs with anything from picking a mentor to choosing a product just because people you associate with suggested it. Doubt is something to absolutely watch out for. Make sure you go forward by taking action and picking the right people in your life.

To connect with Ace Reddy, please visit:
http://www.acereddy.com

BETTER SELLING THROUGH STORYTELLING

John Livesay

John Livesay, aka The Pitch Whisperer, is a sales keynote speaker and shares the lessons learned from his award-winning sales career at Conde Nast. In his keynote, "Better Selling Through Storytelling," he shows companies' sales teams how to become irresistible so they are magnetic to their ideal clients.

I connected with John Livesay over email, through a contact of mine by the name of Shawn. Shawn coordinates his speaker's group and helps sales professionals like Neil Rackham and Daymond John with their professional speaking careers. John Livesay has given keynote speeches on sales for Fortune 500 companies like Coca-Cola, Anthem Insurance, and many others. I was very honored to be able to interview John.

John tells us that sales is when two different people have the ability to connect and communicate a problem in such a way that someone is willing to pay for a solution. The old way of selling was to push out a lot of information and hopefully win the sale. The new way of selling is to tell stories. John suggests turning case studies you have with your company into case *stories*. So instead of pushing out the information, you're going to pull your customers into your story.

The big change we want to see happen in sales is to stop thinking about your monetary goals. Stop thinking about how much money you need to make per month. Instead, start thinking about the cause, as well as why you are selling this specific product. Ask yourself these three questions: *How can I help my customer? Which customers need my product right now? Am I qualified to sell this product?* Figuring out the answers to these will get to the core of why you are selling this product. This allows you to explain your story in a very authentic way to your customer.

We know that people buy from others they like and trust. Trust comes from the gut. The handshake, for example, came about from showing someone that you didn't have a weapon in your hand. You need your customer to trust you. Liking someone comes from the heart. The better you can explain a customer's problem, the more they will understand that you have empathy, and the better you will sell. Now comes the head. This is when your customers will ask themselves, "Will this work for me?" It goes in that specific order: from the gut, which is trust; to the heart, which is liking someone; and to the head, which is the sale.

John's jaw-dropping sales story was when he was selling publications and working with GUESS Jeans. Instead of merely pitching the product, he started out the conversation with two words: what if. John was able to get into the head of the customer, future pace them, and see if they could collaborate together. John asked GUESS Jeans, "What if? Because it's your thirteenth celebration, and it's our fourteenth. We could work together to try to come up with something special for the publication." GUESS got to thinking, and they said, "Wow, that sounds great. We'd love to put a specific GUESS model on every other page in your publication." John got the sale by being unique with the offer he and GUESS collaborated on.

Out of four hundred salespeople in the entire company, John won the salesperson of the year award because he came up with a product solution for a big customer that was exceptional. John also helped one of his construction clients win a $1 billion contract with the Pittsburgh airport. They were up against two other competitors. The construction company was told they had one hour to give a presentation on why they would be a good fit for the job. This was important because they were going to have to work together with the airport for the next sixteen years. John turned a case study into a case story. He helped them craft a good story with four key elements in it. The exposition—which is the script where a picture is being painted of the situation—then the problem, the solution, and the resolution.

The company talked about how they had helped a previous customer. They had their construction crew on site, and everything was done on-time, but the vendors were kept on call in case something went wrong. After the project was done, sure enough, there was a blown fuse. Their vendors were on call and got the situation fixed. The project was due at 9:00 a.m. and the last finishing tile went down at 8:59 am. Since then, their customer had had a 15% increase in sales because of their project. Due to the 15% increase, they had made a dramatically impressive increase in their sales.

Your pitch is the story that helps take your customer from where they are to where they want to be. What's great about telling stories is you can tell them for all of the different parts of the pitch. For instance, you can tell a story about your product as well as your inner team. In the previous construction example that John used, there was a man that was a part of the team who used to build Legos. He was very methodical and meticulous about how he would put things together through the construction company. There was another man who used to be in the military, and with that background, everything he did was done on time and to its fullest extent. Telling stories about the different team members also gave the customer a very strong sense of confidence for them to win the project.

Stories are defined to make your company and your pitch memorable. It doesn't matter if you're pitching before or after your competitors. Some people may want to come first to grab the most attention or go at the end to be the last remembered. But when you tell a fantastic story, you will always be remembered. When telling your story, make sure you also turn it back from yourself to what's in it for the client.

Stories are fantastic when you're in competition with others in corporate sales in B2B or consumer sales with B2C. You will always have competitors. A lot of corporate customers in this day and age are required to get three bids before they make a decision, and in the B2C market, there are new competitors consistently. It is extremely important for you to be able to separate yourself from everyone else. One of the best ways you can do that is through storytelling.

When you're in a competitive situation, storytelling allows you to avoid your product and solution from becoming a commodity. When you become a commodity, price is always going to be the deciding factor, and it's very tough to be competitive in today's marketplace. We live in a time where clients and customers see pitch after pitch. You need to become memorable to them by utilizing storytelling. When your clients remember your story, they can tell it to others and become an ambassador of your product. Potential customers might talk about you to their higher-ups in a corporation or possibly to a spouse or partner as a personal customer. John encourages you to tug at people's heartstrings, so you can pull out their purse strings ($). Create a connection and a memorable experience allowing them to open up their wallets.

John has two great pieces of actionable advice. One is to stop selling and start telling stories. Tell stories about yourself and why you're in business, why you're selling, and why you're doing what you're doing. Also, tell stories about other clients that you've been able to help out. Customers will insert themselves into the story, thereby going on the sales journey with you.

The second piece of advice is about how to go from being invisible to the customer to being irresistible. These are explained as moving up rungs on a ladder. Invisible means customers haven't heard of you. The next rung of the ladder is being insignificant, which is when you don't even matter to the customer. The next rung of the ladder is interesting, which is just merely being in the "friend" zone. The fourth is being intriguing, in which the customer is interested in your product, but they're still not buying it. And the last rung is being irresistible. The top of the ladder is where your customers become raving fans. The way you move from one rung of the ladder up to the next is through storytelling.

John leaves us with one of the most unique sales strategies I've ever heard, regarding selling yourself to get hired. Along with storytelling, one of the things you can do when you want to sell yourself is to future pace yourself to a company that's looking to hire. Ask them one simple question: "When I get hired, if I exceed all of your expectations, what will your life or business look like?" This will keep the conversation going. It'll get the customer or employer thinking of what even greater results could be possible. This tells the client that you're interested in doing more than just what's on the table. Lastly, you'll set yourself apart from the rest of the competition.

To connect with John Livesay, please visit:
https://johnlivesay.com

HUMANITY IS STORYTELLING

Nic Fitzgerald

Nic Fitzgerald has worked on fourteen feature films, two television series, many commercials, and was a freelance photojournalist for the NBC affiliate in Salt Lake City. Now, he is a storytelling marketer, and his focus is on helping businesses and entrepreneurs find and tell their stories.

N ic Fitzgerald is a literal giant. He was a D1 semi-pro basketball player and also worked on fourteen featured films as a storytelling expert. I met Nic through Christopher Vos, who told me that Nic has been an expert storyteller for a long time. This unique skill plays a pretty impactful part within sales. Ever since I started selling, I knew this was one of the most powerful tools to have in your arsenal to be able to win the sale. Stories allow you to connect with your customers. I look forward to showing you in this chapter exactly how stories are used in a positive way to help you win the sale, and to share with you what Nic told us during his interview.

Nic tells us that sales is about forging a relationship with a complete stranger—and all so they can give you money. It's the very start of the relationship that's so important. Sales is extremely vital because it's not only the lifeblood of America but the lifeblood of the world.

Nic was a financial advisor in the beginning of his sales career and only sold products he knew would be beneficial, not just for the customer, but for him as well. Knowing his products would be of use to himself gave him satisfaction that he was being ethical in what he sold. This made him one of the top-ranked sales people inside the whole firm.

Nic explains that you have to believe in and be passionate about what you sell, or you won't be able to sell it. He was in a tough spot prior to his first-ever sale with his personal entrepreneur company, as it had been difficult to make ends meet. He decided to attend a conference called Funnel Hacking Live, located in Orlando, Florida. While the ticket wasn't cheap, he thought it was an amazing conference and money well spent.

He eventually talked to an individual from a chamber of commerce and pitched him a $20,000 project. The service he pitched would have been of great value for the customer, but they countered with an offer to pay zero dollars and to only give him a testimonial. They didn't even want to negotiate on any monetary exchange. This wouldn't work for Nic and his situation.

One of the most interesting parts of the story occurred at the Funnel Hacking Live conference in Orlando. Nic had actually spent $25,000 on an additional program when he was already in a pretty tough spot financially. He didn't exactly know how he was going to tell his wife about it. Nic had met with a woman named Jane at the conference and was able to build a working relationship together. They decided to work on a project which was a $26,000 deal. She wanted to build stories for a course she had. And the interesting thing about it is she didn't even need to see an itemized quote. She just told Nic, "You know what, I like you. I enjoy the style that you use. Let's go ahead and move forward with this project."

Nic tells us about his specific sales methodology: storytelling. At the very core of humanity is storytelling. All kinds of things have been created and destroyed just by telling stories. It doesn't matter if it was drawings on a cave wall back in the day or speaking from stage in present times, we're always telling stories. People have been accustomed to sitting around the campfire listening to stories. In today's modern age, our phones and computers are like our campfires.

Stories allow you to build a connection with a customer. This is when your customer is going to be able to understand your passions and exactly why you're in business, which builds rapport. Your rapport—or story—is used as your pre-frame to your pitch or offer because the connection needs to be made *before* the offer.

For example, let's take a look at the company Apple. Steve Jobs used stories to tell everyone what the world was like before the iPhone launched to what the world could become after it launched. Before, people kept CDs in binders or carried them around on their person or in their car. Dinner recipes would have to be printed out from the web, scanned from a recipe book, or written down on a piece of paper before going to the market. In order to find grocery stores with the proper ingredients to purchase, people got in their vehicle and had to use a Thomas Guide, MapQuest, or Google to figure out the directions to those places.

Steve told stories about how he could revolutionize these certain aspects of life instead of focusing on the features of his physical product. He didn't focus on the Apple iPhone having a three-inch diagonal screen, 56 gigabytes worth of memory, and a A5 core processor, but instead focused on the stories of how people would benefit. He wanted to connect with his customer on a deeper level.

For instance, how would you feel having a disc binder full of fifty CDs that had to be placed up on the dashboard or in the backseat of the car? How would you find the right CD to play for the road trip coming up? That case had been sitting on top of your dashboard, and the hot sun is ruining some of the CDs. Or maybe you've burned a CD and you forgot to label it, so you don't exactly know what songs are on there. Perhaps you're on a much longer road trip and you're trying so hand to pick the best CD, but you've got a disc jacket full of CDs where you can't find the exact one you want to play.

Steve Jobs used stories like this to be able to connect with the customer. He'd ask, "Have you ever run into a situation like this? Have you ever had that feeling where you pull that CD out of your disc jacket and it's melted? Or have you pulled the wrong one from your disc jacket? With the iPhone, or even the iPod beforehand, you'll be able to have thousands of songs that will fit right in your pocket. No struggle and no mess." He was able to connect with customers in that way. And the same thing goes with using a Thomas Guide with maps: "Have you ever been fumbling around with a Thomas Guide and realized you got on the wrong road? And now you have to pull over to the side of the road and figure out exactly how to get to the right location. Did that make you late for your daughter's dance recital? Did it make you late and miss your date? Was your wife or your husband upset because you weren't at the meeting location on time?"

Or perhaps with the recipe book. "Did you ever get to the market and forget some of the ingredients in a particular recipe? You now scramble and try to find what you need to bake that cake; only to find out you missed the key ingredient that you need to make it a success." He used those stories to draw out the emotions of customers and make a connection with them by saying exactly what they needed to hear. He then explains what they could have in the future.

Stories are so powerful that they will allow you to sell more of your given product or you can sell your product for more money. It's always important to have a good product. But using stories is almost like pouring gasoline on the fire. You can always have a product that will sell, but if you use stories, you can really extract that emotion from your customer. You can sell more, and for more money as well.

Now, when it comes to the structure of the story, you want to begin with the end in mind. Think to yourself, *What do I want my audience and customers to think? What do I want them to feel? What do I want them to do?* Once you decide on your desired outcome it's important for you to work backward.

When we work backward, we need to figure out what the end is, what the middle of the story is, and what the beginning is—what it looks like in that order going forward. The beginning should provide you context while the middle develops the conflict and is the meat of your story. The end is where the success is had. But before that happens, there are a few components that always get removed for intrigue and conflict.

For instance, think about *Star Wars*. When people take a look at the very beginning, they might be thinking about the end goal of the rebels, wondering if they will succeed in destroying the Death Star. They'll know from the beginning that this is the main objective. But the beginning needs to give us some context. The story starts out with *A long time ago in a galaxy far, far away…* It begins with the text scroll of the movie telling us exactly what the context is. Then, the middle of the story starts to develop, where we understand that Princess Leia needs to be rescued. *How do we get her back?* There's a little bit of conflict.

Also, Luke goes through a series of traumatic experiences where he loses his mentor, Obi-Wan Kenobi. He feels like he's out on his own. He has to leave Yoda to go save

Han Solo and Princess Leia. There's a lot of conflict that develops in the middle of the story. At the very end, some of those components are removed. When Luke is flying in to shoot the Death Star, he loses all of his wingmen. But at the very end, success is had; he shoots the torpedoes at the Death Star and blows up the enemy battle station. How did this story make you feel? Did it bring out an emotion in your chest and get you excited?

When you use stories, customers come back again and again. These will be your continuity or residual sales. Apple started off with stories, and now every year they release a new phone. People continually go back to Apple to buy their products. But it's that first story that really sets the trend going forward.

Nic left us with two pieces of strong, actionable advice. First, start telling your stories now. You can use Instagram, Facebook Live, or podcasting if you're a little bit more advanced. Get in the habit of telling stories every single day. Doing so will help you get comfortable with telling your stories to an audience and also allow you to find your specific personal voice.

The second actionable item is to be clear on exactly who you want to serve inside of your business. You need to tell your story to the right audience, and the way you tell it, needs to be in the customer's language. This allows you to better connect with your customers, build up that rapport, and establish a trust factor. For example, if you are looking to sell soda to your customers, you don't need to talk about how healthy and physically fit you are. It's very hard to sell that kind of product to fitness enthusiasts. However, if you're telling your story on how you are physically fit and cut gluten from your diet, and you're selling an exercise program or a health product; then those two would naturally link up.

Nic had one really tough sale that was outside of his business. He was with The Church of Latter-day Saints and went on a missionary trip to Scotland to work on converting people. It was extremely difficult because the legal drinking age in Scotland is much lower than here in the United States, and drinking is almost imbued in their culture. What's interesting is that when Nic went there, he was able to build up connections with certain people. He was successful because he used the power of stories to build up those relationships. This was an extremely hard task and very daunting, but it's also one of the reasons why Nic uses stories so much in his business.

Here are a couple of very interesting tips to wrap up this chapter. When we look at our elders, when we look at people sitting around the campfire, those are the ones that are giving us wisdom through stories. Also, the Bible is one of the most influential books of all time and is a collection of multiple stories. Whether we believe those stories are true or not, they have influenced millions of people. These stories were powerful enough to influence action through people, and the world is a different place because of the stories in that book.

Again, with stories, make sure you explain to your customers what your product is and how it came to be. People will be very interested in your product as a result.

To connect with Nic Fitzgerald, please visit:
https://www.friendlygiantfilms.com

CONFIDENT AWARENESS

When we are just getting into selling and when we have been selling for a long time; it is important to be aware of our "why." As salespeople, we often don't remember the true reason why we are selling. Most of us started in sales only to make a living, so we only focused on making money. I know I was guilty of this.

If you remember, I graduated from college wanting to be an engineer and not a salesperson. I was selling just for a paycheck and nothing more. This, in turn, resulted in extremely low sales and a poor daily attitude. Over the years, I have grown very fond of my customers and my product. The mental shift I had was from selling for selfish reasons to selling for customer results. Interestingly enough, as soon as I made this switch, I became a top-five-percenter consistently in business.

It is important to remember this when we have been selling for a long time. We will naturally become self-focused again and strive to increase our bank account or gain prestige at a company. When we sell for the customer instead of for ourselves, success and satisfaction always come in abundance.

My personal sales career has had these highs and lows, but when I remember to listen to the customer, success is inevitable. These next chapters will remind us why we want to serve our customers and how to listen to them.

THE NEUROSCIENCE OF SALES

Dr. Grace Lee

Dr. Grace Lee is a neuroscience expert and global educator best known for being the founder of Mastery Insights, a career and life coaching firm dedicated to empowering heart-driven professionals to maximize their impact, their income, and reach their highest potential in their business or career. Dr. Lee is on a mission to redefine modern education, teaching men and women how to unlock true vocational confidence and master their professional destinies.

I met Dr. Grace Lee through Chantelle, a mutual acquaintance. Chantelle and I wrote another book together called *Overcoming Adversity and Entrepreneurship* where Chantelle shared her story of how she overcame adversity in her life and business. She also wrote a chapter in a book this year called *Million Dollar Story*. One of the other co-authors was Dr. Grace. I read the first few chapters of the book and was highly impressed with what I saw from both Chantelle and Dr. Grace, so I asked Chantelle to connect me with Dr. Grace.

When I spoke with Dr. Grace, she told me what she does and what sales really means to her. I knew after the conversation that I had to get her on the Ultimate Sales Momentum because it was going to be an extremely beneficial interview. Dr. Grace said that sales is simply a conversation that you have with someone. The purpose of the conversation is to shift the customer's beliefs to get them to make a decision they were already trying to make themselves.

There are some beliefs that can impede a customer making a purchasing decision. A sales conversation is all about getting away from those obstacles. As salespeople, if we're selling the right products, we have an ethical obligation to step up and persuade the customer to buy. If we don't make the sale, our customers' lives will not change for the better. They'll stay the same.

Sales is more than just about money. Sales is truly the vehicle which allows us to serve our customers at the highest level. Dr. Grace said that customers have what she calls PQRS: problems, questions, roadblocks, and solutions. These are on customers' minds 24/7, which can cause them a world of suffering. Although they may not realize it because they've become accustomed to this world. Sales is the vehicle that allows the customer to get over the PQRS. They have problems, questions, and roadblocks; then you need to bring them to the solution.

The salesperson's job is to paint a vision of what is possible for the customer by doing so gently and not with an aggressive sales process. Sales here means that we're going through the customer's PQRS and leading them to their desired outcome.

When I asked Dr. Grace if she had any jaw-dropping sales stories, she told us that the most shocking part of a sale is actually the end result. Sales is really a full cycle, with the outcome after the sale being the jaw-dropping part. Her profession is helping individuals with vocational confidence and desires. She had taken on a client who was in his mid-50s. He was married with a sixteen-year-old daughter, had been in sales for the past seventeen years, was a senior in sales, and didn't really know what he wanted to achieve with his career. He was on the verge of quitting his job. But he was the main financial provider for his family, so he came to Dr. Grace looking for help.

He was trying to find purpose and meaning with his career. After working with Dr. Grace for a few months, he had an epiphany and understood what he was really looking to get out of life. The exciting part of the story was that instead of coming home miserable, stressed, and upset; he came home happy because he knew what his purpose in life was. His daughter immediately noticed a difference in her father. He was not only able to make an impact on his own life, but he was able to positively impact his daughter's life. Dr. Grace's client went from experiencing self-change to becoming a coach for his daughter, helping her figure out *her* purpose in life.

According to Dr. Grace, you cannot have a monetary transaction until you fully understand what the whole lifecycle of a customer is. You need to know not only how to achieve results, but what future outcome they will experience as well. Our opinions as salespeople don't really matter. It's the customers' opinions that matter because they're the ones who are voting with their wallets.

When we ask our customer questions, we do so because we need to be perfectly clear with them that we can help them. It's very important that we communicate to the customers that we can help them. If we can't help the customer, then it's our moral obligation not to take the money even if the customer wants to give us money.

Furthermore, we'll often have different levels of a program. The goal is to get the customer into the correct program. If you think about sales as not just selling a physical or digital product, but selling a solution for the customer, you're always going to get it right. Get the customer into the right program or product.

Dr. Grace's methodology isn't so much of an actual methodology, as it is simply showing up as a human being with the three C's: care, compassion, and curiosity. This is when you're able to transfer emotion and confidence to the customer through the sales process. Dr. Grace believes so much in what she does with vocational confidence that she's able to transfer that confidence to the customers she speaks to. For example, when you go to a doctor's office and they ask you what the problem is, the doctor has so much confidence that they have the solution for the customer that they're able to transfer that confidence, that solution, that emotion to the customer. This gets them on the path to health and wellness.

Care, the first C, is genuinely wanting to ask your customers questions so you can step up and help them. Compassion is where you build rapport by naturally connecting with them. Curiosity allows you to explore the discussion with your customer without being interrogative. With curiosity, you're never going to have to worry about what to say next in the sales conversation. The ultimate goal with these three Cs is to become the customer's best friend or confidant in the most genuine way. The three Cs all intertwine with each other during your sales presentation.

Dr. Grace explains that one of the best things about the three C's is that through human nature, we're all capable of these. They're universal expressions of emotion and concern, no matter how we were raised or what our background is. We're programmed to naturally want to help people, to contribute, and to grow from that contribution. This allows us to be more of who we are and have the impact that we want to have on this world—ultimately creating a big win-win all around.

Dr. Grace gives us two pieces of actionable advice. First, recognize that sales conversations are not about you; they are about the customer. When you realize this, sales conversations are no longer scary. You'll go into the conversation not being stressed out, and you'll be very certain of what you need to say each and every time.

The second piece of actionable advice is you need to get clear on what you believe about sales and wealth generation. If you're not building monetary income or momentum inside of your business, it's truly because of you. It's not the economy. It's not your marketing. It's not your team. As a business owner or professional leader, you need to rise up and take ownership of the decisions that you make.

Dr. Grace has a saying that *your inner world creates your outer world*. This is especially important. There are some key questions you should ask yourself to be clear on what you believe about sales and wealth generation. *What do I believe to be true about sales? How do I feel about sales as an activity? How do I feel about salespeople? How do I feel about asking someone to spend money on my products?* Answering these questions allows us to show up in the best way possible as a business owner or professional.

It allows us to show up each day as an 11 out of 10. In our business, this is especially true if we have team members because we need to be that 11 out of 10, the best model for your team to follow. Your team members will never be that higher number. Being an 11 out of 10 means you'll be the one who understands your own vision and is able to communicate that to your team.

When I asked Dr. Grace what the most important sale she had to make outside of her business was, she responded without hesitation by saying that it was the sale within herself. She dares to say that this is one of the most powerful sales that almost everyone has to make. She had been in academia for a number of years. She graduated as a doctor and then went into the formal education system. But while going through the educational system, they never taught her how to think about the core of herself and what she was interested in doing.

Dr. Grace received three degrees, spent multiple years in college, and was trained in neuroscience. Throughout her educational career, she worked toward obtaining a formal job as a professor. What's interesting is that it just didn't happen. What she experienced happens with a lot of people. Growing up, we're programmed to understand that, after high school, we go to college, get good grades, then get a good job. What happens is the longer we're in school, the deeper these beliefs become. So while she pursued higher education, she wrestled with the idea of going down this path.

Dr. Grace went through academia and into the corporate world, but still felt something tugging on her heartstrings that she was supposed to do something greater. The toughest sale she had to make was to honor that thought and grow in entrepreneurship, even though she didn't have an MBA. She had a PhD. She didn't take classes in economics. She didn't come from a family of entrepreneurs, so she didn't have that in her 'DNA'. She needed to sell herself so that she could do something more on her own.

As Dr. Grace was going through the PhD program, there was a lot of unspoken pressure. Everybody strives toward the finish line, which is getting a faculty position at a university and becoming tenured. But the faculty positions are not as plentiful as the students that are going through the system. I know this myself because my cousin is on a similar path with human psychology. He has his PhD and is trying to find a job at a university but is being forced to travel across the country to universities that have open positions. These positions only open up when a new position is created, where there is a death, or when someone retires.

What Dr. Grace did instead was think about her true meaning and passion. She did the research and actually held seminars inside of the classroom with other students. They were also interested in figuring out other options that would fulfill them within their life and career. There's a movie called *Catch Me If You Can* starring Leonardo DiCaprio. In the movie, he becomes a surgeon, a lawyer, a dentist, and a financial accountant. And when they finally catch him, they asked him how he did all those different things in life. He said, "Well, you just have to stay one step ahead of everybody else." That's what Dr. Grace was doing by teaching others as she learned.

Dr. Grace became passionate with the new role she took on. She was naturally selling through this process and also found a marketplace that had a need within the academia sector. She wanted to help others who were in her shoes and found a market that was receptive to the information she wanted to teach. What Dr. Grace implemented, without even thinking about it, were the three Cs: to care for her colleagues, to have compassion, and to have the curiosity to go further with her teaching. She was able to start a successful business out of it. Her advice is, if you don't sell you on *yourself*, then somebody else will sell you on *their* dreams. And when you get sold on somebody else's dreams, that's when burnout will inevitably happen. You've got to step up and make the most important and difficult sale—selling yourself.

To connect with Dr. Grace Lee, please visit:
https://careerrevisionist.com/masterclass

FROM SCARCITY TO SERVING

Amanda Dake

Amanda provides strategies and tactics to coaches, experts, and business owners that help them grow their businesses online. She has a big passion for helping others make money doing what they love and eliminating uncertainty, frustration, and burn-out while keeping in their own zone of genius.

I met Amanda Dake through Cody Neer, and she came very highly recommended as a marketing specialist. She also trained directly under Russell Brunson, a marketing master. Marketing is a vital aspect of sales. Amanda and I had a very intelligent conversation, and I was excited to have her on the Ultimate Sales Momentum. According to Amanda, sales and marketing boil down to relationships. Relationships are key, especially in the digital world we now live in.

You need to be able to incorporate yourself into your own sales and marketing, which is important when you're talking to coaches and consultants. Sales and marketing are about people and connecting with them. You need to be the solution provider for your customers. When you're providing the solution be open and specific with them.

Amanda's best sales story was when she spoke on stage as she has done so many times throughout her career. Her best moment in sales was when she was able to get her first table purchasing rush after a speech. This means she got a chance to pitch something at the end of her presentation, and the product she pitched was a high-ticket product. After she gave the pitch, customers ran to the back of the room to a table and signed up for her program. This was a great feeling for Amanda.

Amanda realized that the reason she had a table rush was because she connected with people at the event. She had a chance to talk with some of the audience before the event, then talked to them while she was speaking on stage, and talked with them further after she was done presenting. This is what resulted in the great number of sales for Amanda. It was through her connecting before, during, and after the presentation that allowed her to do this.

When you're able to share your own story, you build that connection and trust with customers. So incorporate your own personal experiences into your story. You'll have common ground with your customers, which will allow them to see the results that you have as attainable. They won't see you as above them, and they will believe they can achieve the results you said they would. Tell them exactly what their unique needs are and relate those to your experiences. This will help you in sales time and time again.

Also, never lie to them. If you can't get them results, that would be a fake connection as well as unethical. If you're doing what you're meant to do, then the connections and the people you serve will be very easy and authentic. You need to serve your customers entirely by focusing on them as a whole. Ask them about their personal and professional goals. Get to know them.

Amanda told us about her framework, which she calls "CTA." This is not a call to action; it's clarity, tactics, and action. Clarity is when the customer has that 'lightbulb' moment. When they have total confidence in exactly what they're moving forward with. It's crucial that your customer is clear on exactly where they need to start, so they can begin moving the ball forward. You don't want them to be chasing 'squirrels' or 'shiny objects' and new opportunities. You want them to be focused on *you* and *your* solution. And for them to be 100% clear.

Tactics are simply looking at certain websites, funnel design, email automation, and more. These are the pieces that put the puzzle together. Make it work.

The last part is action—putting the marketing together through YouTube ads, Facebook ads, organic marketing, newsletters, and so on. One key tip is to provide your customers with a roadmap and give them the right tools they need to succeed. Do not leave things to chance for your customers if you've been able to give them only a portion of the solution. If they do not get their desired results, customers will come back and blame you every time. It's only ethical and right to ensure that your customers have success after you've sold them. Also, a lot of people prefer to stick within their zone of genius. This means their expert skills and what they're most passionate about and good at. If you can teach your customers how to get the other pieces, you can ensure that they'll have success after you sold them.

Amanda leaves us with a couple of pieces of actionable advice. One is to get super-clear on what your goals are for your business. If it's a sales quota you're attempting to achieve or a monetary goal you're trying to make per month, see if you can find out exactly how much money you need. Ask yourself the question, *Does this monetary amount correlate to the offers that I have?* Once you're clear on this, you can connect with the people you want to serve and build a relationship, rather than just solely sell to them.

Also, when you get clear on exactly how much you need to make, you can relax. And when you relax, you step out of a scarcity mode in sales and move into a serving mode. When you're not in a scarcity mode and not worried about the number that you need to hit, you focus on your customers. You will make sure they get the quality product and the deliverables they expect. Customers will always know when a salesperson is in need of money and only wants to make the sale. It's very hard to be successful when you're in this kind of mindset.

Amanda's suggestion to relax does not mean stop working or go take a vacation. It's a shift in your thought process from being anxious to wanting to serve. It's about maintaining a constant connection with people rather than selling all day every day.

The last piece of advice is to remember—no matter if you are in sales, run a business, or are selling for somebody else professionally—to always ask yourself three questions: *What do I want to do? Who do I want to serve? How much money do I want to make?*

To connect with Amanda Dake, please visit:
http://www.amandadake.com

THE BRAND CONNECTION

Malena Southworth

Malena is a military spouse, mother of three, a believer, and an expert in branding and website design. She got her start at the award-winning marketing agency Bulldog Drummond and served as creative director for the Suz Somersall jewelry line for seven years before embarking on her own entrepreneurial journey with her branding and web design studio, Southworth Design Co.

I had the pleasure of speaking with Malena Southworth, who is a specialist and expert in branding—as well as a military spouse.

Branding is a crucial element of sales. If you can't brand yourself properly, then it will be very hard to convince people to buy your product. Your brand needs to represent you and exactly who you are.

Malena taught us that sales isn't something you have to trick your customer into or that you have to shove down their throat. It's as simple as inviting somebody to check out a product you have, which they'll be able to benefit from. When breaking down sales, this just means starting a unique relationship with a customer. Think of sales as a first date. Every relationship is unique to each and every customer. With branding, really listen to your customer. Ask them questions so they'll tell you exactly what your brand needs to be. Again, it is vital that you listen to your customer and start the relationship successfully.

As you're building the sales relationship, you want this to be something where you can work back and forth together with the customer, like you would with dating. You're going to have the initial phone call or the initial point of contact, but just like dating within relationships, you have to go on multiple dates or experience it multiple times with the customer. Have that back and forth interaction and figure out the best way to work together.

Malena was kind enough to take us through her procedure with branding. Do this in the very beginning of your business if you can. Build your business around what your target customer is and what you want to portray yourself as, rather than building your business around what you think your customers wants you to have. To reiterate, build your business around who your customers currently are and who you are yourself; not what you think your customers want to see.

What can help you with this in the beginning is putting together a mood board. This mood board should have pictures collected from Pinterest, Google, magazines, or other resources that describe who you are at the core. An exercise you can do is to go to Pinterest and pin pictures to your board or download images from Google every single day for five days straight. Eventually, you will see similarities with what you're trying to portray. This will give you a great idea of what your core brand needs to be. The mood board should represent yourself as much as possible, that way your company is a representation of you.

Let's say you're thinking about how to decide on a brand and want it to be described as classic. Now, when you or a branding specialist thinks classic, that can mean different things—classic retro, classic vintage, or classic guitars. You need to be specific.

The second part of the procedure is to find adjectives and adverbs that describe you and your business. This way you have both pictures *and* words to use together, painting a complete picture of your specific brand.

Malena was kind enough to take me through a branding exercise herself. I am a licensed US Coast Guard captain and have always wanted to start my own recreational, small side-hustle fishing business. What I would do initially when getting into branding is portray myself correctly.

I'd go to Pinterest or Google and pick out certain images that resonate with me: the boat, somebody having fun, blue skies, and some rough seas. Next, I'll pick out some adjectives and adverbs as well: long nights, patiently waiting in anticipation, excitement, and rushing. Many of these different words are going to help paint a picture of exactly what this company needs to be.

I know I'd want to portray something of excitement, but there's also some anticipation and fear of loss because that's how fishing can be. Additionally, pick out the right colors for your specific mood and what you want your personality to depict. Mine would be blue and white for the oceans and the sky.

Malena ran through this exercise with a customer who had a fitness business and wanted to portray herself as super strong and motivational. She picked very intense colors and graphics, such as red and black, which can come off as highly stern and emotional. But her client was caring and gentle, wanting to create a relationship with people to understand what their core needs were. She didn't want to be portrayed as a drill sergeant, but as warm and compassionate.

In this example, neutral colors like blue, gray, or white may have been a bit better instead of strong and powerful colors like red. Representing herself as very motivational and gung-ho in that manner resulted in clients being shocked at the person they were experiencing when they invested in her program. It didn't match up. She was able to rearrange her branding, making sure the message portrayed was what clients experienced when they went to see her in person. Eventually, the business was up and running, had the correct branding behind it, and became very successful.

Malena gave us two pieces of actionable advice. The first one she really wanted to drive home is to listen to your customers. One example of when she did this was around the Christmas holiday. Customers were requesting a product that she didn't have. It was as simple as listening to them and understanding exactly what they wanted. If you don't have the product, you can create it for them and make a very easy sale.

The other piece of actionable advice is if your customers are telling you to pivot a bit in your business, make sure you can become flexible. Serve them at the highest level because sometimes they'll tell you that you need to take a bit of a different direction. We're all in business to both serve our customers and sell to them. As long as it's ethical and you desire to serve your customers in this way, you can go down that different path and pivot.

Malena had one very difficult sale outside of her business: trying to get her child to eat vegetables. It was quite a struggle to get him to eat vegetables because he only really enjoyed rice and carbs. But he was also intrigued by dinosaurs. While she's not proud of this, she told him that a triceratops eats leaves, and if he ate salad greens and vegetables, he might grow horns like a triceratops. Her son gobbled down vegetables and ate salad for months, checking the mirror daily to see if he had grown horns. Malena ended up having to tell him that he wasn't going to grow horns. This is a good lesson because if you lie to your customers by telling them they'll get good results that they're not actually going to get, it doesn't do any good in the end. Unfortunately, her son still struggles with eating vegetables, but Malena was kind enough to share the story with us because of its lesson.

That's why branding and sales are so important in your business. Take the steps we covered in this chapter. Listen to your customers. Have them tell you in the very beginning of business exactly who they are as a person. Figure out what kind of customer you want to attract and put pictures and adjectives up on your mood board. This will lead you to your unique specific brand.

To connect with Malena Southworth, please visit:
http://www.southworthdesign.co/must-haves

LISTEN AND SERVE

Andrew Izumi

Andrew is an action taker, independent thinker, and leader in sales strategies. He has been a leading sales manager for over a decade, having achieved certificates like Leading at Emerson, a Fortune 500 company.

What is sales and why is it important? Sales is possibly the single most important skill in life and in business. This might be selling your first product to a customer, or maybe it's selling your spouse or your children on eating vegetables. Sales truly do make the world and your life go round.

This is why we really need to expand upon this skill and take a deeper look. Sales, by one definition, is the process of getting something or someone from point A to point B. It is filling the gap.

Sales means much more to me than just money. It means focusing on the customer, giving them exactly what they're going to need, so they are happy after being sold. It is proving to your customer that your product will get them the desired result which they need. It is also following up with them after you've sold them the product to make sure they're happy, and they have received every single result which was promised.

One amazing sales experience I had was with a customer named Jim. Jim was one of the best and most loyal customers I had ever had. He consistently placed orders of $10,000 to $40,000 like it was nothing. The jaw-dropping part of this sales story is that, after the product had been proven and the first sale was made, he was a customer for life. (And still is to this day.) This happened because of two activities that were done consistently after the sale was made.

One activity I do is consistently call and visit the customer, while asking questions about our service and listening to the answers. The company I was working for at the time was not perfect. Orders were missed frequently, and pricing mistakes were made as well. Jim would tell me exactly what was going on, which made it very easy to listen and correct the mistakes we had made. If I had neglected to follow-up and ask questions, he would have stopped purchasing our product.

The second activity I do is promptly act on tasks that need to be taken care of. I would go above and beyond the call of duty to make sure that Jim's requests were taken care of immediately. Many times, I would over-deliver to assure him that his business was highly valued. This led to him being honest and loyal.

Have you ever heard the saying that all buyers are liars? By listening and serving your customers, you can ensure that your customers will instead tell you the truth. Jim would even tell me when my competition was trying to steal my business away. He would assure me that nobody was going to take away my business as long as I was around.

The specific sales methodology that I use is called the 'sales call triangle'. I use a triangle because it is the strongest geometric shape, having three equal sides. The first side of the triangle is listening. Listen to the customer and hear what their problems are. Do they need delivery to be a bit faster? Something more robust? What exactly are their specific needs? The more you listen to your customer, the more they will tell you exactly how they want to be sold. As long as you can accommodate them and be the solution provider, you will be a successful seller.

The second side of the triangle is connecting. No matter how much you listen, it doesn't matter how great your product is if you don't receive any trust. Try to find a personal connection. Go out for a drink with them or be genuinely interested in their family. Look for common interests even outside of business. Build a relationship, and that will build trust. Customers need to trust you before they buy from you.

The third side of the sales call triangle is speaking. Speaking is where the pitch comes in. Have your pitch down when telling customers about the features and the benefits. Tell them how those features and benefits will transform their life. Paint a picture of what their future will look like after they purchase your product or service. Also, make sure to speak to the pain you are removing for them.

It comes in that order: listening, connecting, and speaking. There are a lot of sales methodologies out there, but if you remember these three simple steps—no matter if you're doing business online, in-person, or selling to big corporations or solopreneurs—it will work.

Here are three pieces of advice that will skyrocket sales in your business. The first is to make sure to ask your customer at least three questions at the beginning of the conversation. Here are some examples: Why did you want to get on the phone with me? How can I best serve you today? Maybe even just ask how they're feeling. *Remember, if it sounds like they're not having a very good day, maybe If it's not the right day for you to be on the phone, and it would be better to reschedule that sales call.*

The second piece of advice is to find out what their end goal is, the result they truly want. You might say something like, "I know we have a product that possibly might be a solution for you, but I would like to know what it would mean for you when our product is successful."

The third piece of advice is to sell to people you enjoy serving. Passion and sales go hand in hand. If you are not selling something that you would use yourself, customers will see this and not buy. When you are passionate about your product, it will also keep you an ethical seller. Salespeople often get looked down upon, and this is because there are many salesmen who are very self-serving. Be proud to serve your customers, and be ecstatic about your product. Customers are very smart, and when they see your confidence and passion, it will naturally instill belief in them leading to a purchase.

In this book, my goal for you is to be able to see all the different sales methods and the different mindsets behind them. Sales is a unique skill and also an art. You'll enjoy connecting with this group of experts who will get you to the next level. I want you to find the systems which you are really drawn to and implement those within your business.

Finally, once you've conquered one mountain, you can move on to the next, and then the next, incrementally getting better and better. This is how to keep blowing past that plateau you may be experiencing in your career. This is what the Ultimate Sales Momentum is all about. It's all about getting you unstuck from wherever you are. Whether it's in the very beginning and you're trying to make your first dollar, or if you're at $1 million and you don't know how to get to $2 million.

The most difficult sale that I will have is selling each reader of The Ultimate Sales Momentum. I want to help out every person who has the privilege to receive this material. There have been endless nights, weekends, and vacation days writing and thinking about the best way to present this information to each and every one of you.

A win for me is for you to experience a dramatic change in your career and life. These experts and methodologies have dramatically changed my life for the better, and I trust they will do the same for you.

Please let me know what epiphanies you have or big wins. I would love to hear how you have succeeded. Or, if you are stuck and want help getting over the sales hump, please email me at: andrew@ultimatesalesmomentum.com

Thank you and enjoy the remaining two bonus chapters.

To connect with Andrew Izumi, please visit:
www.andrewizumi.com

BONUS CHAPTERS: ONLINE AND IN-PERSON TACTICS

There are two very powerful sales methods that I wanted to touch on: online sales and in-person sales during live events.

Online sales have exploded through the power of the internet. Whether you are selling through Amazon, eBay, or other stores, this style of selling is powerful and will remain so for many years to come.

Live event sales are also extremely important because, in a virtual world, we often get unplugged from the live interaction that is so critical in sales. Personal interaction and a handshake can never be replaced.

Myself and all of the chapter speakers have used both of these sales methods to some degree. Learn these essential tricks and techniques to compete and win online and at in-person live events.

CONNECTING AND FACILITATING [E-COMMERCE]

Cody Neer

Cody Neer has a knack for online advertising and marketing and started turning heads and catching the attention of world-class brands including Target Corporation and Shark Tank's Kevin Harrington, both of whom hired Neer to help drive sales for their online stores. With results like $350,000,000 generated from $56,000,000 ad spend, Neer quickly used ecommerce to gain his own ticket to financial freedom,

I reached out to Cody Neer when I realized we were going to attend a mutual conference. The conference didn't end up happening, but I was still able to make a connection with Cody since it was a small event. We had a conversation about sales, which led to a future conversation about fishing.

I got a chance to talk to Cody about what he does in his e-commerce business because I was very intrigued at how much money he has sold over the web. This turns out to be over $400 million in e-commerce over the past few years. I knew he had a sales system in place and asked him if he would be interested in being a participant of the Ultimate Sales Momentum. This led me to find out how he was able to sell so many high-quantity products over the web.

Cody said that sales is simply figuring out who your customer is, and then where your customer is looking to buy. Your job is to connect the two and give them what they want to buy. Cody also wanted to share with us a jaw-dropping sales story.

Cody has two sides to his business. One side involves selling physical products to customers, and the other side teaches individuals exactly how to start their own e-commerce business on the web. This relates to his second business. There was an individual who decided to invest in his program, which was $60,000 for a single year. While that's a very large investment, the 62-year-old man wanted to go all in and make a commitment of trying to get a source of recurring revenue for himself and his family.

The individual was a bit hesitant about spending the $60,000 but as soon as he did, he saw results right away.

In his first year he sold $100,000 worth of products. Over the following years he brought in $25,000 per month in net profit. He was able to make back his money and gain a positive ROI, return on investment, very quickly. This allowed the man's wife to retire, then he quit his job, and now he focuses solely on his e-commerce business. He sells kitchen islands, grills, and the kitchen sink. You know how people say you sell everything except for the kitchen sink? This man sells everything *and* the kitchen sink!

Cody's sales methodology for e-commerce products is extremely unique. He takes a direct relationship approach, meaning he'll go directly to the supplier or the manufacturer and build a relationship with that company. This places him in a unique position as opposed to his competition. He negotiates a win-win situation with them in terms of what his commission—or commission percentage or payout—will look like for each specific item. This is because he can talk to the supplier on the phone. This type of methodology works so well because he is one of the few e-commerce businesses using this strategy.

Next, Cody simply puts the product on shopping sites such as Google Shopping, Bing Shopping, or Amazon. When you can sell a product that has a good reputation like General Electric or DeWalt, you can leverage their credibility and significant reputation in the industry. Then, you just place the product in front of a certain number of customers, and the law of averages kicks in. You're able to use General Electric or DeWalt with their many years of established SEO, search engine optimization, to sell your products.

The second way of using this sales methodology is to also—along with SEO—use paid traffic. This allows you to get your specific product in front of the right person who is looking for it at that point in time.

When choosing a specific product to sell, there are two simple rules. We already talked about one of them, which is using brands that are notable in the industry such as General Electric, Nike, Adidas, etc. You could also sell top-dollar products. For example, a General Electric refrigerator is probably going to cost more than a Walmart t-shirt.

It is also recommended to choose products that are not seasonal. For instance, if you pick Christmas trees, they're only in season once a year for a short time. But if you pick a different product, such as refrigerators, you can sell those throughout the year.

Cody explains one other critical fact: e-commerce really boils down to the law of averages. If you pick the right product and get in front of the right person, the law of averages will kick in. It'll allow you to win over time. It's kind of like playing card games in Vegas casinos. What most people don't know is that card games in Vegas are actually designed for the customers to win. But in Vegas, the house plays the law of averages against the players because they know that seven out of ten people will make knee-jerk decisions by betting big when they're not supposed to.

Another tip is to pick products that people will need again and again. For example, Cody says that if you pick products that a plumbing contractor will need to purchase, such as sinks or refrigerators. You can leverage the fact that they will come back to you again and again for each job they have. Keep selling that product, especially when you're able to negotiate a specific price or a specific agreement with that manufacturer, such as General Electric. You can then give those contractors a really good price. This will give you an extreme strategic advantage when you have to compete with stores like Lowe's, Home Depot, Target, and others. These stores have to pay for a physical location and employees. They also have other overhead finances that you will not have in your e-commerce store.

One of the best strategies you can leverage is actually picking up the phone and having a relationship with that supplier, which will provide you with a strategic advantage in your business.

Now let's talk about what to sell, and this is very simple. When you're selling things online, sell necessities, not accessories. Accessories are what people either shy away from or make as impulse purchases. But if you sell necessities, you'll have customers repeatedly coming back to you. The continuity is what's going to build a reliable and strong business.

The last two pieces of advice Cody gives us is to always have good customer service for your products. Build a brand, and your brand will reflect exactly how you treat your customers. Do you pick up the phone when they have an issue? Do you provide support for them on the website? Do you take returns on products that aren't working properly? Amazon is a good example of having built such a great customer service reputation. Their customers know that if they have Amazon Prime and order something, the items will be delivered within two days. Customers also know that if they have problems with the items they buy, they can return them within the first 30 days with barely any questions asked.

The second piece of advice is not to be afraid to pick up the phone and have a conversation with somebody. You not only want to speak, but also listen, because the person on the other end of that line will give you the answers to the questions you have. You need to understand exactly what they're saying by *listening*.

One of the hardest sales Cody has had outside of his traditional e-commerce business is building systems for himself. These systems are built so his e-commerce businesses can be self-sustaining and continue running after he has given up the day-to-day work. Cody finds a lot of joy in finding the SOPs, standard operating procedures, the specific strategies and tasks that need to be done daily. When he builds a business, it will endure without him actually being there. This is one of the hardest things he's learned, but also one of the most satisfying.

To connect with Cody Neer, please visit:
https://ecommercebrandacademy.com/

ATTENTION AND RETENTION [LIVE EVENTS]

Chantelle Cotton

Chantelle Cotton is a master event and sales strategist/coach and motivational speaker with over eighteen years of sales experience and a proven track record to follow. She teaches entrepreneurs, small business owners, and corporations how to increase their revenue by closing more sales before, during, and after an event.

Chantelle Cotton is an expert sales stage closer, who Jim and Cindy Padilla connected me with. They recommended me to Chantelle because they knew she could close from stage and had actually been doing some sales closing for them during some of their live events. She came very highly recommended being that she had already worked with the Padilla family.

I was very excited to be able to talk to Chantelle about how she is able to close sales. What we learned from her is that sales is simply a conversation between two people trying to get to a common solution, and that sales is the backbone of every company. It's all about teaching people what to say, how to say it, and who to say it to. If you can figure out those three things, you will become very impactful in sales.

One of the other foundational pieces in sales is you always have to remember to ask for the sale. Do not assume it will happen and that your customer will pay you. This is actually one of the biggest mistakes people make. You must be proactive and ask for the sale.

There was one time when Chantelle's customer was very afraid to ask for the sale. Time and time again, she went through the sales process and didn't make any money. She would give a lot of value but never ask for a sale. Eventually, she was able to lead a customer to a sale and was asked by the customer how much it would cost to get into her program. She replied that it was $30,000. This allowed her to pay her bills for months. But at that point in time she realized that she couldn't expect customers to continuously ask how much they needed to pay for the service she offered, and she needed to be much more proactive.

Chantelle teaches that there are five specific steps to the sales process. The first step is to build rapport. You need to make that connection with the customer. The second step is fact-finding. Ask them questions to find out a little bit more about them, their business, what their pain points are, etc. Third, get the customer to answer their own questions. When you can get them to give themselves a response to their own questions, with the solution that you provide, you lead them down the road to success with the product that you're trying to sell.

The fourth step is to paint a picture of the future for your customers. Tell them exactly what it will look like when they get a chance to work with you. What is their goal at the end of the road? You want your customers to identify what they're going to achieve after they've already had success with your product or program. Finally, step number five is to ask permission to share with them your specific solution before you ask for the sale. It's extremely important to listen to what the client needs because you don't want to give them what *you* want, you want to listen to them and feed off of the exact information they give you.

One of her key tips is not to be attached to the outcome, meaning don't be so attached to just gaining and winning the sale. If your customers aren't ready to purchase, then it's essential that you use follow-up because not everybody is ready at the time the pitch is made to purchase your product. If you follow up with them, you will understand when the right time will be. Also, if you're not attached to the outcome and don't push the sale, your customers may refer you to one of their contacts who they know is ready for your product.

Chantelle explained that to sell from the stage, there are three main parts. The first part is letting the audience know right from the beginning that you have something to pitch them. You do this so they're aware of what's coming. This prepares the audience throughout the entire presentation and helps to lead them to an offer at the end. That way your customers come into the presentation expecting something to be delivered at the end.

The second stage is telling stories and teaching. This is how you'll keep your audience engaged. You want to have your audience remember exactly what you're able to teach. You do this through stories.

The third part is to present your offer. There are a couple of key tips to provide that offer and to successfully drive the sale home. Have a sales team at the back of the room. The team is designed to have individual conversations with clients to give them more information and answer any personal questions. The pitch can go many different ways, but each individual person is unique. They're all going to have a different situation and different questions regarding that specific pitch. Some statistics indicate that 95% of the people in the room will have those extra questions they really need answered on a personal level. 5% will get what they need from the presentation and will be ready to buy without any additional information.

This is why it's essential to have a back-of-the-room sales team so you can capture as many sales as possible. This team is also responsible for fitting the right program with the right person. In many events, there are multiple programs that offer everything from a beginner's-level program to an expert-level program. It's vital to be able to get the correct individual matched up with the program best suited for them.

For instance, if you have somebody who's a little more advanced and they've already gone through more of the beginning stages, don't pitch them a $1,000 program if they're ready to spend $50,000. Conversely, don't pitch a $50,000 program to the person who has recently gone into business and is dipping their toe in the water. They may buy into that at first, but not have the money to do it. Additionally, it could be so accelerated for them that they may not know exactly what to do. In both of these situations, make sure people are partnered with the exact program they need. If you don't do this part of the procedure, then failure is inevitable. And with that failure, you don't get any referrals or recommendations—and without any success, you don't have a long-term sales strategy.

It's critical we discuss how to go about positioning the specific event, which pertains to structuring certain pieces of the presentation during your live event. What's very interesting is that a person only retains about the first twenty minutes of any given presentation. This means your presentation should be broken up into sections, especially if you have long days or it's a multi-day event. Give people time to use the restroom. Typically, convention centers are cold, so attendees will be drinking warm coffee, maybe tea, and you don't want to have them miss the presentation to use the restroom.

Another hint to remember about breaks is that, once you give them the offer, have them go on break so they have time to sit down. They may chat about the offer with their business partner, friend, or spouse. If you keep teaching after the offer is presented, you'll likely detract from whatever the offer is, and they won't have a chance to think about it and potentially buy.

One thing to keep in mind is that people are very resourceful. If you've made a good offer pitch, and if customers do not have the money, a lot will try to figure out exactly how they can get it. They can use something like CreditWise, PayPal, a relative, and so on. During that time, they also have a chance to talk to the sales team. Remember, each person is unique with their own set of specific questions. Give them the opportunity to approach the sales team with concerns about financing to see if they can work out a payment plan with you. Sometimes they will have questions about the phases of the program they will go through.

Make sure not to pitch at the very end of the event. For a single-day event, make your offer toward the early afternoon or shortly after lunch. If it's a multi-day event, think about pitching on day two instead of day three so you can give yourself ample time before the event is over to re-pitch after you've given them a bit more information. Do yourself a favor and give them another time where they can go to the back of the room, put their credit card down, and invest in your program.

What's really unique is Chantelle's team makes an excellent effort to create a connection with each and every person that comes to the event, which is unlike anything I've ever seen before. This is so specific in that attendees know where they need to go if they have questions, so they're not stumbling for the answers or going to the presenter themselves. They know they can go to Chantelle's team and get these answers.

Pay special attention to the close during your live event. Seven to ten days after the close is made, Chantelle's team follows up with the customer. For those who didn't purchase the product, don't ask why they didn't buy right away. They might have needed more time to think about it. People will go back home, talk to their spouse, or maybe they need to get their finances in order. So it's extremely important to follow up seven to ten days after the event.

Another interesting thing about the close is that, after the customer purchases the product, it's very beneficial to have some sort of celebratory lunch or dinner before the end of the event. You don't always know exactly what everyone's travel plans look like, so do this before the very last day. For the people who weren't able to purchase the product, they will see that there is already some action moving forward for the people who have purchased it. The attendees are having fun and already receiving a benefit from their purchase, and they're already starting to get the promised material. This prevents buyer's remorse and refunds. This is called a stick strategy because you're ensuring that when people make the investment, they are continuing their momentum.

The last part is to have a retention team for the people who have purchased your product. And again, we do want to make sure that we get the right product into the right person's hands. For instance, you don't want to sell somebody a $50,000 product they weren't right for and end up having to downsell them. Have your retention team give that person a call and say, "Hey, you know what? We could sell you this $50,000 product, but at this point in your business, you're really best suited for our $5,000 product. We still have the intention of getting you to the $50,000 one, but right now you should have this product."

Even though you are losing money, this can prevent the risk that the customer may request a chargeback on their credit card and cancel their membership or program. Also, when you accelerate your customer through the program at the correct pace, they will probably end up purchasing that more expensive product in the future. Similarly, if you are selling to somebody who is at a more advanced level, and they need a more expensive product, you might want to have that conversation with them and say, "You know, you've already purchased your $5,000 product. We really think you're ready for the $50,000 product. Is there any monetary obstruction in the way? What exactly is the situation with finances because we know that you can become successful." You don't want to have that customer come into your program at the $5,000 price point, not really get what they need, and then not go through the remainder of the program. You can't assume they're going to accelerate at the rate you know they need.

With the physical positioning of the event have it in a location with warm weather, like Florida or Southern California, rather than somewhere cold during the winter. Also, have it somewhere that's very easy to fly to, like Washington DC during the spring, Los Angeles, Florida, etc. This way people can come from, not only within the United States, but all over the world.

As far as the positioning goes for the specific event inside the room, have the tables designed in a way so that the presenter isn't untouchable. Think about how a roundtable setup would look versus stadium seating, where the audience might feel like the presenter's on a pedestal. Thoughtful seating arrangements provide more of a community aspect, and it's more inviting for people to approach the presenter and the team. They'll likely be much more willing to buy into the program because they feel like they're a part of the family.

There are two pieces of actionable advice that Chantelle gave us. One is to survey your audience and ask them what they need. Be clear on exactly what your customers want, as well as exactly what you will offer them. If those two do not meet, it'll be very hard to get people to your event and for your attendees to purchase the product. You'd be surprised at how far off you can be with what you think your audience wants. Instead, survey exactly what their intentions are from a live event.

The second piece of actionable advice is to have a stick strategy to make sure the attendees actually show up to the event. Don't do marketing any longer than six months before the event, otherwise people will forget about it. Although emergencies do happen that could prevent some from attending, keep them engaged through email sequences and possibly even physical gifts delivered in the mail.

Be very aware of the total cost for the event. In the beginning, block off a set of rooms. If you don't get a lot of attendees coming in and filling up those rooms, you will be stuck with that bill. This also includes catering, how much food to order, and the cost of the event space. If you don't have people fill the event or you purchase too many rooms, you may pay for more than what you'll be able to upsell or receive on the back end.

Chantelle remembers one difficult sale she had. As a side hustle, she sells health insurance specific to cancer. She had one customer to whom she was trying to sell insurance. During the conversation, she knew they were definitely on the fence as to whether to purchase the insurance or not. They told her, "I don't know if I can really buy this insurance because I feel like I'm just going to jinx it."

Chantelle said, "Well, there are really two ways that this can go and either way, it's totally up to you, and I support your decision. One way is that you purchase the insurance and you're covered, not a worry in sight. The second is you have the possibility of having to worry about what happens if you were to get cancer. What position do you want to be in?"

It was a very simple question, but they said, "You know what? I really value the comfort, and I understand it, and I think it's a wise decision." The individual decided to purchase the insurance, which was a good move because, unfortunately, they ended up having stage-two breast cancer. But they had purchased the insurance and were taken care of. They're alive and well and monetarily burden free today. So whether Chantelle is closing at a live event or closing a single person on an insurance sale, she uses those closing strategies to help get the customer to where they need to be while both positively impacting them and herself in the process.

To connect with Chantelle Cotton, please visit:
www.chantellec.com

BUSINESS ALPHA AND OMEGA

In business, sales is the first and last activity you should focus on. Before you even create a product, it is crucial to understand how it will be sold. That market or customer base needs to be understood, and it is your job to take this to market and solve a problem. This ensures that sales can be accomplished.

Every person inside of your business is a salesperson and should be selling 24/7, 365 days a year. Sales never quit, and each individual on your team is a contributing member to your salesforce. This goes from the person who loads boxes in the trucking dock to the digital marketer who runs your YouTube ads. Every individual plays an extremely important part in solving your customer's problems so the business can keep cash flowing.

The strategies explained in this book have not only worked in the 21st century but throughout history. Sales was the driving economic force even during the Roman Empire. Julius Caesar became the first dictator of Rome by selling his people on the much-needed reform of the great city, Rome.

In summary, remember that sales start even before you interact with your customer and continues all the way past taking their money. Sell your initial concept, sell your product and solution, and continue to sell during the follow up ensuring that the customer's result has been achieved.

I look forward to you implementing these teachings and exploding your sales beyond where they are today. If you take consistent action now, I can assure you that sales momentum will pick up speed moving toward a very successful future. Thank you for reading, and I wish you exponential success!

For the full video interviews, please visit

www.ultimatesalesmomentum.com

and watch the in-person interaction.

The Sales Call
TRI∆NGLE

1. Listening

- Ask your customer questions about their current situation and problem
- Listen intently to their answers, which will help you craft the close

2. Connecting

- Place yourself in the customer's shoes and become empathetic
- Build trust with your customer by establishing a relationship beyond the product

3. Speaking

- Pitch your product by explaining how it can help achieve the desired solution
- Include a vision of what a successful future will mean to your customer

Find a deeper explanation of Andrew's methodology on page 115.

ABOUT THE AUTHOR

Andrew Izumi

Andrew is passionate about sales. Through his lifelong experience, he wants to share his knowledge and interviewed expert's advice. Learning from others and passing this information along is the best way to keep growing. Sales is truly one of the most beneficial skills to have in business and in life.

Andrew wants to see others succeed quickly. A world with better salespeople will lead to many more important problems being solved. One of his goals is for you to become a salesperson to whom customers desire to speak.

Enjoy the knowledge ahead from centuries of successful professional experience. Andrew would love to hear about your wins and epiphanies or if you have any sales questions you would like answered.

Please connect with him at:

andrew@ultimatesalesmomentum.com

THANK YOU TO OUR EXPERTS

THANK YOU TO OUR SPONSORS

A special thank-you to our sponsors for making *The Ultimate Sales Momentum* possible:

JETLAUNCH — High-quality book design and publishing. jetlaunch.net

The COPY CIPHER — Writing jaw-dropping copy. thecopycipher.co

NICHOLAS DODGE — Building sales funnels that convert. nicholasdodge.com

MIRAJE GRAPHICS — Designing graphics that inspire. m.me/MirajeGraphics